ENTREPRENEUR?
Bring Your Vision to Life

The Guide for Christian Entrepreneurs
to Turn 'What if?' into Reality

Ralph McCall

destinēe

Copyright © and 2006 and 2011 by Ralph McCall

Originally published in 2006 as, Bring Your Vision to Life. The 2011 version has been updated with new material.

Without limiting the rights under copyright reserved above, no part of this publication may be reproduced, stored in, or introduced into a retrieval system, or transmitted in any form or by any means (electronic, mechanical, photocopying, or otherwise), without the prior written permission from the publisher, except where permitted by law, and except in the case of brief quotations embodied in critical articles and reviews. For information, write: info@destinee.ch

Reasonable care has been taken to trace original sources and copyright holders for any quotations appearing in this book. Should any attribution be found to be incorrect or incomplete, the publisher welcomes written documentation supporting correction for subsequent printing.

All scripture quotations, unless otherwise indicated, are taken from the HOLY BIBLE, NEW INTERNATIONAL VERSION®. NIV®. Copyright ©1973, 1978, 1984 by International Bible Society. Used by permission of Zondervan. All rights reserved.

Published by Destinée Media, www.destineemedia.com

Cover design: Per-Ole Lind
Cover image: psdGraphics
Editor: Anna Elkins

All rights reserved by the author.

ISBN 978-0-9759082-2-8

Table of contents

Prologue   1

Introduction: Bringing Your Vision to Life   5
Day 1: You are a vision builder, an entrepreneur   10

Action One: Identify Your Vision   14
Day 2: What is your vision?   15
Day 3: Search within yourself   19
Day 4: The pressures that may stop you   23
Day 5: Your vision: Is it worth it?   27
Day 6: Goals and age groups   31
Day 7: Your story   35
Day 8: Vision and faith   39
Day 9: Reframing your vision   43

Action Two: Establish Your Map   46
Day 10: The cartographer   47
Day 11: The Legend—Your plan   51
Day 12: Domain—Who and What?   55
Day 13: Compass—Where?   59
Day 14: Tools and choosing them—How?   61
Day 15: There is a bottom line   64
Day 16: Money: Beneath the mattress?   69

Action Three: Manage the Stages with Wisdom   72
Day 17: Setting the Stage(s)   73
Day 18: Essentials for Tasking   79

Action Four: Set and Achieve Targets   83
Day 19: Targets and dates   85

Action Five: Be Accountable   87
Day 20: Confide and consult   89
Day 21: Keep your secrets   91

Action Six: Take Action   94
Day 22: Act now!   95

Action Seven: Get the Spiritual Implications   97
Day 23: Distinctive service   98
Day 24: In the spirit   103

Conclusion
Day 25: Sum it Up   106
Into the journey   109

Recommended Readings   111
End Notes   112
Destinée Media   115

ENTREPRENEUR?
Bring Your Vision to Life

PROLOGUE

In the midst of all personal and economic circumstances it is possible, with God's leading, to bring your entrepreneurial dreams and desires to life. If those desires are God-given, it means the result will be something positive in the world.

But to bring your vision to life it means you need to define it, put a plan in place and then take the necessary actions to make it happen. And it involves faith. That is the process outlined in this book.

Entrepreneurs come in many forms, but to be one most often starts by asking the question that begins, "What if . . . ?"

What if I started a cooperative baby-sitting service in my church? Or a new ministry or humanitarian work?

What if I started a new business: high-tech? Or, a bed and breakfast?

What if I got out of debt?

What if I did something with my retirement freedom?

What if I changed something in my life?

What if I did something about the needs I see in the world?

For a destitute family of nine in a Manila shanty town, the question began when the parents asked themselves: What if we could provide education for our children? They put all of their energy into helping their oldest son through law school. He in turn supported his next sibling through university, and together they helped the rest of the children complete degrees.

This was one form of an entrepreneurial act, at a family level. It started with "What if?", and turned into reality.

The interesting thing about being an entrepreneur is that the "What if?" can be asked at a multitude of different levels, from the individual to the family, to the neighborhood, to the city, state and world. This can cover everything from people and products and every other aspect of the world around us. . We all have these dreams, for it is a God-given part of our nature, to imagine, to create, to fulfill needs and make things better.

#

But what if your dreams and desires can be stolen?

I know a husband and wife who own a home in the suburb

of a large American city. They each hold well-paying nine-to-five jobs and live comfortably. Early in their marriage, they set up a retirement plan and have saved to help their children through college. One child is in her second year at university and the younger boy will be going as well next year. The family is pleasantly ensconced in church life as are all of their friends.

Doesn't sound too bad, right?

I met this couple for dinner. After long descriptions of their plans for a tropical vacation next winter, they admitted feeling that they are missing something.

"Earlier in our marriage," the wife said, "We had a passion to do things like start a bed and breakfast, lead mission groups in Mexico, or take our kids to New England to see where their great grandparents lived."

Her husband nodded and added, "But it's hard to be dynamic once jobs, kids and mortgage get in the way."

Or did they allow those things to "get in the way?"

#

I also know a college student in his third senior year. He changed majors a few times and then decided to take half the normal credit load to have time for fun. On an average afternoon, you can find him playing Internet games at his computer. In the evening, he's likely slumped into a worn 1950's sofa with a television remote in one hand and his chin in the other, watching reruns of old TV series.

The last time his parents called, he hung up the phone, angry that they expected him to know what he wants to do with the rest of his life. "How am I supposed to know what to do with my life?"

Even as he remembers asking that, he knows he should be doing something. And not just getting a job. Once, he thought it would be great to find the cure for cancer or direct films or something. He senses that there is a greater calling in his life than the various monitors he sits in front of.

I can relate to that college student. I was somewhat like him years ago. And that student is out there today, in all shapes and sizes.

These two scenarios are not isolated. Both result from fear. The couple is afraid they might lose their well-planned life if they venture to try something new. The college student keeps changing majors because he is afraid he will miss his passion if he settles on any one thing. He sees so many options out there, and he's afraid that if he picks one, it will turn out to be the wrong choice and a failure.

#

Fear isn't the only reason that dreams go unfulfilled. People get caught up in habits and living in secure routines. The couple started a life like all of their friends: job, kids, house, taxes, exotic vacation every so often. Now they are trapped serving routines that come with those responsibilities. Even the student elected to take an early "retirement" into a secure routine that limits his life.

And then there are internal mental patterns at play. The college student is driven to apathy by the belief that "nothing I can do will make a difference." He is haunted by doubts and low self-esteem. The couple is constrained by a cerebral box they have built around themselves. The result? They can't think outside of it.

How about you? Do you have a feeling in the pit of your stomach that your life could be more? Do you have a desire to change your life or the life of others for the better? Maybe you've settled into a decent but unfulfilling routine.

Maybe you have robbed *yourself* of your dreams.

Realizing this is a good starting point. You're ready for a vision.

#

But there's another consideration in thinking about the couple and the college student. It's something that impacts every living person on this planet:

We live in an economic reality, constantly reconfigured.

It's a universal truth that goods and services need to be produced for humans to survive and advance. This reality presents a constant challenge. Yet, what was today's economy will not be that of tomorrow.

Even though the couple lives in their economic "security", is it really that secure? Well paying nine to five jobs come and go. One's house and other assets can be devalued from one moment to the next.

And the student is living in a dream world if he thinks he can live on mommy's handouts forever. Things will change.

As the world moves through continual cycles of prosperity and recession (even depression), there are always enormous opportunities for new goods and services. Many of these originate from entrepreneurs who pursue the realization of new ideas.

Some of the world's largest and most successful companies and humanitarian organizations were started in bad economies.

#

Is the economic reality shifting underneath you? Do you see human needs that demand fulfillment?

Are you ready to articulate your vision and see it realized?

INTRODUCTION:
BRINGING YOUR VISION TO LIFE

Your vision
What are your dreams and desires? What are your recurring imaginings or wishes of how things could be that, if fulfilled, would make a significant difference in your life and the lives of others? These lead us to your vision.

What is your vision?

Can you answer this question? Articulating your vision is often difficult, but I want to help you do just that. Because if you can identify your deepest, God-given desires, narrow them down to their essence, and plan for their realization, you can bring them to life.

This declaration comes from someone who grew up in Southern California and then found himself working everywhere from professional basketball courts between Asia and Israel, to University in England, to the United Nations in Switzerland, to a seventeen-year stint with a large, multinational company.

I am a Christian and this book is presented thorough that lens. If you have a different way of seeing the world it is my belief that you will still benefit from the principles you find here. I took a long and individual path to living my faith. That path included many dreams—both realized and not. Along the way, I have certainly learned a few things that could save you time and serve as guideposts toward the realization of your own dreams.

I challenge you to stop and think about the things you want in your life or the lives of others. If you don't, you may get stuck in an unfulfilling routine, and life may just pass you by

There are as many visions as there are eyes
The founding fathers of the United States of America had a vision to create a new kind of country; Jonas Salk had a vision to eradicate polio, a group of researchers at CERN, the European Center for Nuclear Research near Geneva, Switzerland, had a vision to connect the world through the Internet. These are indeed remarkable visions.

But visions don't all have to be

on grand political or economic scales. You can have a vision of returning to school to finish your Bachelor's degree, of helping at your local soup kitchen, or of improving a relationship with your parents, children, or partner.

Visions fall into one of two categories: doing something new in an existing context and doing something new in a new context. The first category might involve making a needed transformation in an existing situation within your company, political structure, church, athletic club, or family. And the second might entail changing your profession entirely and following a yearning to become an artist and influence people with your art, or to start an environmental awareness program in your community. At the heart of both vision categories is an internal awareness that what you are currently doing is not what you were created to do.

Whether it is to start helping out in your church office or to start a new commercial enterprise, your dream can look vastly different from anyone else's.

But your vision will share one thing in common with everyone else's: it will create a passion in you to bring it to life.

Without a vision the people perish

Proverbs 29:18 states quite bluntly that "Without a vision the people perish."(KJV)[1] As in: no vision equals death. Visions are not just pleasant mental images to keep life interesting during a long commute. They are necessary for life.

What is your vision? Simple enough question, but can you answer it this second, in a couple of sentences?

Maybe it's not so easy. It can be "easier" to get caught up fulfilling the daily expectations of the world around you with all its bus schedules, lunch meetings, family outings, paper deadlines, bill payment, social engagements, gym time and so on. I completely understand that most of you rarely have any free time to think about your vision, let alone to pursue it.

Or maybe you can state a vision, but it feels borrowed. If your vision sounds half-hearted, it is coming from your head, not from your heart. Often this is because other people have handed the vision to you—teachers, family members, social groups or simply anyone who has made you feel you "should" be pursuing something. In this sense, others are writing your life story.

Even when your vision does come from your heart and you have a passion for it, you may doubt or fear pursuing it. If your vision is different from the expectations of people around you, are you afraid to go after it, or even to tell others about it?

When you acknowledge a vision that is your own, be prepared to begin one of the most rewarding experiences of your life. Don't allow a fear to block this process. Yes, you may be disappointed along the way. Yes, you may encounter seemingly immovable obstacles. But you *can* move them. Moses stuttered and was afraid of public speaking. Yet God used him to lead his nation to freedom.

#

After all of this you may be asking, what exactly is a vision? I'll expand on this definition later, but for now look at vision as a vivid mental picture and goal for how things can and should be. Vision is a passion that drives you forward and gives your life and actions both purpose and meaning. I believe that everyone can have a vision because everyone has dreams and desires.

Your path

The purpose of this book is to help you state your vision and work through bringing it to life. When you are finished, you should be able to actively pursue an endeavor that will bring a positive change to the world around you, add a greater sense of fulfillment to your life, and help you become what you were meant to be.

To help you identify and pursue your vision, I have broken the process into seven actions needed to achieve a visionary goal.

The necessary seven

Your path will take you through seven actions I have established for the journey. I will walk with you as you learn to:

1. **Identify your vision**
2. **Establish your road-map**
3. **Manage the phases with wisdom**
4. **Set targets and achieve them**
5. **Be accountable**
6. **Take action**
7. **Comprehend the spiritual implications**

The principles at the core of each action have emerged from a variety of sources. I have spent years working with numerous entrepreneurs with their even more numerous adventures. I have conducted my own academic research on the successful implementation of business plans and visions. I have taught courses and seminars on entrepreneurship in graduate schools, international organizations and church groups. I have spent countless hours listening to and coaching people toward finding and doing what matters in their lives. And I have also tried to achieve my own personal goals.

Probably like you, I have experienced both failures and successes.

As you take each action, remember that you are moving toward the heart and core of your vision.

Changing the system

In the seven actions of this guide, I look at vision from the perspective of innovation and redemption. I support my approach with concepts originating in the study of entrepreneurship.

When some people think about entrepreneurship, they do so in terms of an economic perspective, as in: starting a company to make money. But the most basic definition of an entrepreneur is "someone who changes the system." Broadly speaking, "the system" is the way things are done in your life and in the institutions around you. More specifically, I take that a bit further and call the entrepreneur a vision builder: "someone who changes the system *in a positive way*." That's what a good vision will end up doing — making a change for the better.

I believe that there is a bit of the entrepreneur inside all of us. We all have the capability to change the system in a positive way. For many people, that capability is unrealized potential.

Using this guidebook

To help you bring your vision to life, this book contains a fair number of questions for you to answer. Don't just fill in the blanks. Give honest reflection to each question.

To make it more personal, go get yourself a special journal or notebook that feels good to you. Use it to write down your answers, make notes and brainstorm your ideas. As you work through an action you may gain new insights that will cause you to retrace your actions. Stick with it.

#

I have written this book in the casual tone you would experience were you sitting in one of my seminars or consulting with me one-on-one.

Whether you are working through this on your own, or with a study group, spend adequate time on each action and subsection. Plan to spend one day or more on each chapter.

At the website www.visiontolife.org you will find helpful resources to complement this book. They are there to enrich the foundation laid in this book.

#

Now, I cannot be strong enough about the next statement:

To get the most out of this book you must deeply consider and answer all the questions as you move through each of the seven actions.

Don't skip any question. Don't rush it. Reflect on each question during the day, or over many days if necessary.

This is serious business. It is the business of vision-building.

DAY 1
YOU ARE A 'VISION-BUILDER', AN ENTREPRENEUR

I never perfected an invention that I did not think about in terms of the service it might give others . . . I find out what the world needs, then I proceed to invent.   Thomas Edison

Before moving into the seven actions, let's look at some principles from the field of entrepreneurship—or vision building, as I like to call it. This particular chapter may seem a bit slow going and I can understand that you want to get into the practical steps of starting your project. But first it is very important that we build a theoretical foundation. The purpose is, you need to continually understand what you are in the context of building your vision.

You also need to recognize that there are different types of entrepreneurial projects.

#

Let's start with the word 'entrepreneur.' Many people stumble over this word and feel it does not relate to them or their vision. You might be surprised. Take a minute to answer the following two questions:

1. **When you think about the word 'entrepreneur' or 'entrepreneurship,' what do you think of?** What are entrepreneurs to you? What are their characteristics? What are their qualities?

2. **Do you think of yourself as an entrepreneur?**

Once you identify your vision and begin to pursue it, you have in fact become an entrepreneur. Reflect on the following definition:

Entrepreneurship is the process of identifying, developing, and bringing a vision to life. The vision may be an innovative idea, an opportunity, or simply a better way to do something.
The Entrepreneurship Center at Miami University of Ohio[2]

What is entrepreneurship?
The word 'entrepreneur' originated in France around the seventeenth century as 'one who is enterprising' and 'one who

is charged with executing certain work for others.' *Entre* means 'to enter,' or 'to be between,' and *prendre* means 'to take.' So combined, the word can literally mean 'to enter and take,' or 'between-taking,' or 'go between.'

'Entrepreneur' is also linked to the French word *entreprenant*, or 'enterprising.' This describes someone who is bold and audacious or one who is daring in an enterprise. One who builds a vision.

Originally, the word 'entrepreneur' was used by French economists Richard Cantillon (1680-1734)[3] and Jean-Baptiste Say (1767-1832)[4]. Since the time of Aristotle, economic activity and entrepreneurship were seen as something of a lower order. But Say and Cantillon argued that entrepreneurs held valuable roles in the equilibrium of supply and demand and they provided a significant role within the economic system.

#

Their idea was later extended when Joseph Schumpeter (1893-1950)[5] defined an entrepreneur as someone who uses innovation to destroy the existing economic order. While this sounds negative, Schumpeter meant it in a positive way. In other words, economic systems will stabilize to the point where they become stale and begin to deteriorate, but the entrepreneur will come along and interject new products and services into the system, thereby destroying the old order and renovating it.

#

In 1890, Alfred Marshall described the entrepreneur as the one who provides innovation and progress.[6] And in 1961, David McClelland went even farther by suggesting that entrepreneurship accounts for the advance in civilization by providing the entrepreneurial spirit that exploits those resources.[7]

So you can see a dramatic evolution of the concept: from being looked down upon, to not only fitting within and contributing to the economic system, but advancing it.

'Self-centred' vs. social entrepreneurship

It is a misconception to say that entrepreneurs are self-centered and self-serving or that they just want to create personal wealth. One website paints this unflattering picture of an entrepreneur:

"An entrepreneur is a person who starts a business to follow a vision, to make money, and to be the master of his/her own soul, both financially and spiritually."[8]

While entrepreneurship can create wealth, this definition is limited. To attempt to be the master of one's own soul is a flawed philosophical view of reality that leads to anything but freedom. And, there is nothing wrong in creating wealth, but if the emphasis of one's endeavor is only to make money, the endeavor paradoxically loses meaning and is devalued.

Most recently the term 'entrepreneurship' has expanded beyond a pure commercial/economic context, and it is common to speak of 'social entrepreneurship.' A social entrepreneur perceives a social need or opportunity and is able to develop activities or an organization to meet those needs.

Entrepreneur as an agent for positive change

Once the idea of social entrepreneurship rubbed shoulders with the idea of commercial entrepreneurship, the term broadened and generated more definitions.

Harold Shapiro defines entrepreneurship as, "any activity whose objective is to change the system."[9] This echoes Shumpter's model of entrepreneur as someone who destroys the system.

In a similar definition David Johnson states that, "An entrepreneur is an individual who takes initiative; who assumes responsibility and ownership for making things happen; is both open to and able to create novelty; who manages the risks attached to the process; and who has the persistence to see things through to some identified end-point, even when faced with obstacles and difficulties.[10]"

I propose that entrepreneurship—vision-building—is one expression of what it means to be human. To be human is to be created in the image of God. The world is a fallen order in an ongoing state of deterioration. We need innovation in the commercial world to change and advance it, and likewise we need innovation to restore and advance all areas of life. Individuals, families, and personal relationships need healing. The environment needs innovation and redemption, as does our political world. The opportunities for entrepreneurship are enormous.

Building a vision is a redeeming and innovative activity with the purpose of restoration. While all entrepreneurial activities are likely to have economic components, entrepreneurship goes beyond using a set of economic techniques to create wealth.

Now we have a working definition: an entrepreneur is a vision builder who *identifies, develops and brings a vision to life in order to change and advance the system through innovative redemption.*

Still, that's a bit of an academic mouthful so to simplify things remember Thomas Edison. He sought out what the world needs and then proceeded to invent it, always thinking about the service it might offer to others.

#

We are called to be agents for positive change. To be vision-builders.

Question

1:1 Seen within this context, ask yourself the question from the opening of this chapter again: Do you see yourself as an entrepreneur?

Now let's move on to the seven actions:

Action One ▶
Identify your Vision

DAY 2
WHAT IS YOUR VISION?

One of the most provocative facts I know is that every man made object, as well as most actively in your life and mine, starts with an idea or picture in the mind. Catherine Marshall, *Adventures in Prayer*

Before you answer the question of what your vision is, make sure you fully understand what I mean when I use the word "vision."

"Non-visionary" vision statements

Just like 'entrepreneur,' 'vision' means different things in different contexts.

Take organizations. Having vision is one of the core qualities of a good leader. It is also part of the overall strategic planning process and often expands to become the 'shared vision,' of a group collectively developing a picture of the future.

You've probably heard that many organizations have a 'Vision Statement.' This is typically a short sentence or two describing what the organization wants to achieve. If you were to read a typical organizational vision statement, you would probably think it sounded rather dry—like a set of objectives rather than something passionate originating from the heart. Here is the vision statement of one large company: "Our vision is to be one of the top companies in our industry in the next five years." This does not come anywhere near the heart of what that company really wants to be. What is that 'special' thing it wants to be?

Beyond its business and management contexts, vision exists on an individual level. Counselors and personal coaches use the word 'vision' to get their clients to define what they want to be. An example of a personal vision statement:

"I am in better physical health, finished with my studies, actively involved in a close personal relationship, making time for leisure activities, worshiping and serving God daily, and making twice as much money as I do now at a job I love. "

This personal vision is somewhat like that of the business vision statement I mentioned earlier. It sounds more objective-focused than visionary. It fails to get to the core of its author's being. It doesn't inspire anyone to rise above present circumstances and make a difference.

Both of these organizational and personal 'vision statements' are banal. Who is inspired by a mere set of objectives with no transcending purpose?

A vivid mental picture
Dictionaries define vision quite differently than the banalities above. To paraphrase Merriam Webster, vision is:

1. A religious or mystical experience of a supernatural experience

2. The act or power of seeing or imagination

I get much more motivated to think of vision along these lines. Here you finally find the focus on things mystical and supernatural. Nowhere do these definitions sound like a mechanical systemization of a set of corporate or personal objectives like those we saw before.

A vision is a vivid mental picture born in your imagination. It elevates us toward a grander purpose in our lives.

An ecstatic beholding
To truly understand the meaning of vision, it is helpful to see how the word is used in the Bible. The most frequent usage occurring in the Old Testament is the Hebrew word, Hazon חזון, which translates to 'an ecstatic beholding by the seer.' As the Proverb I mentioned earlier told us, "Where there is no vision *(hazon)* the people perish."[11] So that could read, "Where there is no *ecstatic beholding by the seer*, the people perish."

Vision also arises in the context of divine revelation and appearance. While theologians hold dissimilar views on such things, I'd say it's easy to agree that an ecstatic beholding by a seer is considerably different from the mechanical methods used to create corporate vision statements. Vision is more than a defined target to be met in three to five year's time.

You must be passionate about your vision and not treat it like another idea to be broken down into a master plan. While the vision may indeed involve planning, note that its origin will be a vibrant experience, an imagination, a vivid mental image. This is what will motivate you to carry it through.

Origins of vision
Where does a vision originate? From sensing your own or someone else's need, from a personal interest, a perceived opportunity,

or through a feeling that something needs to be changed in the world around you. Such were the circumstances for the following visionaries:

In the mid 1800's, Geneva businessman Henri Dunant took a trip to northern Italy. On 24 June 1859, he arrived at the scene of the Battle of Solferino, one of the largest and bloodiest military battles of that century. Countless wounded and dying soldiers lay on the battlefield with no one doing anything to help them. Back in Switzerland he started The Red Cross, which eventually established standards for the treatment of wounded soldiers and prisoners.

In 1955, African-American Rosa Parks refused to give up her seat to a white passenger and was arrested. Her desire for justice kicked off a movement that ended segregation in the United States.

Nelson Mandela had a vision for living in a country where every adult could vote.

Walt Disney had a vision to create a place where both children and adults could go and have fun and use their imaginations, so he created Disneyland.

In 1976, Anita Roddick started a shop to create a livelihood for her family. But she had a broader vision. She wanted her business, The Body Shop, to encourage social and environmental change. It became a global operation employing and empowering thousands of people.

At a time when most computing was done on corporate mainframes, Steve Jobs and Steve Wozniak had a vision for a personal computer to sit on every office desk.

Martin Luther King had a vision for a country where children of different races would receive the same educational advantages and would be able to play together without intolerance.

Each of these visions came from a different source, yet each visionary saw a need and answered it with an imaginative action. Several of these visionaries share another thing in common: many people perceived them as stupid or crazy. In fact, many of these ideas received resistance from others.
    That's something you will most likely have to face with your vision. Your vision is something you believe in, but others may not.

Be prepared for people to call your idea (or even you) ludicrous or wacky.

#

As you can see, visions come from a variety of sources. Their origins are as diverse as society itself. If you feel blocked when trying to imagine what your vision might be, consider the following starting points for visions. You might:

- **Have an idea for new products or services**
- **See the need for a new process or better way of doing something**
- **See the needs of others**
- **Notice that changes are needed in the institutions or organizations you are a part of**
- **Envision opportunities of various kinds**
- **Seek to improve relationships amidst family, friends, community, or nations**
- **Realize your own personal interests and needs**
- **Acknowledge the need for a personal change**

Your world is full of opportunities of all kinds at all levels. But there is likely one thing that will stand out from the rest, one that you would love to spend an entire day doing. It might already be nudging you to pay attention to it. Now you are ready to begin identifying it.

Question:

2:1 Can you envision your ideal day? What does it look like from waking to sleeping? Be as specific as you can. Don't worry if it sounds silly or serious, impossible or simple. What would you spend an ideal day doing?

DAY 3
SEARCH WITHIN YOURSELF

Your vision will become clear only when you can look into your own heart. Who looks outside, dreams; who looks inside, awakens.
                              Carl Jung

Whether you are nine or ninety you can have a vision that you feel passionately about, a vision that pulls you forward. It's like having a goal you can't resist moving toward.

I don't have a vision

You might be saying to yourself, "Nope. I don't have a vision. There is nothing that motivates me." I protest. Most people have a vision because most people would like to improve something in their life or someone else's. Most people want to make an aspect of life better.

Remember that Proverb: "without a vision the people perish." Could this imply that without a vision we are among the walking dead? Without getting off onto tangents beyond the purpose of this book, I'll simply say that some of today's theologians interpret this verse to mean that without a God- inspired revelation, the people will have no direction.

Now don't start to feel guilty if you can't identify a vision yet. As I mentioned, all people dream of betterment to some degree. On the simplest level, people see something they would like to change in their lives or in the world around them.

Start by searching within yourself

A good starting point for identifying your vision is to begin by searching within yourself. As the publisher and businessman Malcom S. Forbes said, "The best vision is insight."

Ask yourself questions and spend time writing down your thoughts and answers in your notebook. Some suggestions:

- What am I most passionate about?
- What am I good at?
- What are my core competencies?
- What can I be the best at? (Not what do I wish to be the best at)
- What is my personality: introvert, extrovert?

- **What do I enjoy doing?**
- **Where do I see need in the world around me?**
- **What is it that I really want to do?**

In the process of answering these questions, it is important to submit your search to God, involving his insight and direct leading. Ultimately what you're after is what you are called to do. Your calling can be difficult to recognize because it's closely tied to your identity—knowing who you are, how you define yourself, and your unique qualities. (If you desire to investigate this further, I would suggest reading *Courage and Calling*, by Gordon T. Smith.)

#

Since we do not have the imagination God does, we may allow our insecurities or prejudices to turn us away from our potential. Jonah didn't even like the people God was telling him to evangelize. Sometimes God has purposes beyond the abilities we think we have. As Saint Teresa of Avila warned: "God gave us faculties for our use; each of them will receive its proper reward. Then do not let us try to charm them to sleep, but permit them to do their work."

Don't let yourself get caught in the trap of thinking "I don't really know myself that well." Or "I'll just wait until I have a clearer picture of the future." The future is never that clear and often we discover our being through our doing.

Your vision is already there
Your vision has likely been waiting in your heart for some time. It is an idea that you continually keep coming back to.

One woman had a desire to be an artist since she was young. But her family told her she could not make a living with her paint brush and that she should teach instead. She suppressed her dream and did as they suggested. She taught grade school for years without passion, except for the times she was able teach her students art.

Finally, she acknowledged that she had been deceiving her heart. This awareness helped her reaffirm her original desire, and it set her on a new path that led to the fulfillment of that initial, internal call.

Your vision is already there, but for various reasons, it has been marginalized and needs to be recalled. But know that the process of achieving that vision may involve your attention over months or years. That's a small investment for changing the course of your life. So begin searching for possibly dormant desires already residing in your soul.

Am I being selfish?

Time and time again, I talked with people who have started to identify their vision but have internalized the message: "I am being selfish." Visions most often involve some element of personal goals, and when we desire something for ourselves our internal critic says, "You should feel ashamed for wanting this for yourself." On the contrary, your vision will probably have many beneficiaries, including yourself. Yet for many people, when the slightest element of self-fulfillment and satisfaction enters the equation, the equation cancels out.

For our immediate purpose of identifying your visions, call off the critics. Don't worry yet about whether or not your vision is "selfish." We'll deal with this later. Just do some judgment-free brainstorming. When management consultants use brainstorming to generate ideas for a project, they stress that no idea is wrong, and no one is to object or criticize the idea during the process. Categorizations and analysis are made later.

Get going

At this point, I'm going to ask you to seek out your vision. To open your thought process a bit, I would like you to answer three questions. Your answers may not be definitive, but they will begin to trigger ideas. Whatever you do, don't worry about the wording or 'validity' of your writings. Your main objective for now is simply to put ideas on paper.

Questions:

3:1 What are your dreams or visions? Write whatever comes to your mind: things that you strongly feel should happen, the things you dream, things you want changed. Put aside for now suggestions that family and friends have made. Include as many details and descriptions as occur to you. (Your answers may be vastly different from the final vision you develop.)

3:2 What is your most important vision? Go through your list. Remember that a vision is a vivid mental picture of how things could be for you and others in the future. Which vivid picture holds the most importance in your life?

3:3 Write your vision statement: In about fifty words or less, write the first draft of your vision. You will probably be reworking it in subsequent chapters, so don't worry about getting it perfect.

3:4 What is stopping you from achieving your vision? Make a list of the things that are keeping you from achieving that vision.

DAY 4
THE PRESSURES THAT MAY STOP YOU

The man with the new idea is a Crank until the idea succeeds.
                    Mark Twain

In the last chapter you began to identify your vision as well as some of the things that are holding you back from achieving it. From my experience, many people will change their vision idea after a day or two, after they have spent time thinking about it. Don't worry if you change your idea several times. Getting to the core dream in your life can often take time.

Your vision is outside your normal boundaries: Keep in mind that your vision often places you in entirely new territory. It may move you toward things and circumstances that you have never experienced before. Your vision is outside your normal patterns and boundaries. We live in a world of routines, and your dream is most likely beyond those routines. It presents a new reality for you.

You need to be willing to take risks and step outside existing boundaries. Those boundaries are much more complex than a two-dimensional box drawn around you—what you may visualize when you hear someone say "think outside the box." Many dynamics constrain and keep you from moving forward to pursue your idea. Do any of these sound familiar?

The rat race and daily grind: Ah, the demands of life. How do you pursue a dream when faced with all that school, work, family, church, social responsibility, and so on? Each element involves ongoing challenges that you must face on an individual basis. These take up your time and mind. Once one problem is solved, another pops up and yells to be dealt with.

Even the ancient Greeks understood this. The mythological character Sisyphus got to spend eternity pushing a rock up a hill only to have it roll back down. And then he had to push it up again. At home you do four loads of laundry today, and tomorrow the hamper is full. At work you find replacements for a missing shipment today, and tomorrow twice as many are needed.

These daily responsibilities and pressures need to get done. But they can hinder you from moving forward to achieve your vision by demanding all of your energy.

The corporate ladder: In the work world, you may be caught up in climbing the corporate ladder, or just hanging onto your rung by meeting a stack of new objectives your boss handed you.

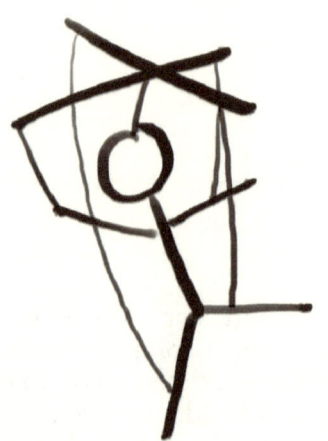

Society's pressures: Then there are the social systems. These contain paradigms — written or unwritten rules that establish constraints about what you 'should' and 'shouldn't' do. If you come up with a new idea that is seen outside the established norms, those around you may call you or your idea wacky. Social systems around you can be resistant to the changes brought by your vision.

Thought processes: You also have to face the doubts and fears in your own head. Everyone has those internal gears grinding, "I can never do that, I shouldn't take the risk, I'm going to fail, I don't know what the outcome is really going to be, it's going to impact the relationships with the people I know" and so on. Don't underestimate the power of those recurrent negative messages that may even sound legitimate. All of this negativity keeps you from stepping out and going after that vision.

Multiple ideas: I don't know if you are like me, but often I get many ideas that go something like: "Wouldn't it be cool to try ..." or "... would be a great opportunity." Such musings are part of the creativity process. The problem is that one idea replaces another, which replaces another, ad infinitum. Nothing ever really gets done. Or if it does, it doesn't fit a more comprehensive theme in your life.

So your vision sits out there, but one or all of the dynamics above might be holding you back from achieving it. It's important to realize that these constraints are at work all the time. If you don't identify the ones in your own life and deal with them, you will not be able to bring your vision to life.

Question:

4:1 Which of the above constraints (or others) weighs most heavily in your life and why?

DAY 5
YOUR VISION: IS IT WORTH IT?

The power of love that called forth the universe, calls on us to create, too – not out of nothing, for only God can do that – but with what the Creator has given us.   Madeleine L'Engle

I want to remind you that your vision will require your time and energy, both physically and mentally. Before pursuing your vision, walk with me through this valuable exercise. You are going to run your vision through an eight-question filter. I suggest this for two reasons. One is to ensure that your vision meets certain criteria to determine its merit. Two is to help you understand your real motivations for bringing your vision to life.

1. Does your vision provide a service and how?

A janitor who cleans an office building each night is providing a service to the workers in that building. The banker who protects and invests someone's portfolio is providing a service to a client. And the homemaker who runs the house and nurtures children is providing a service for his or her family.

Service is evident in most work activities, and so you will likely be able to identify a service component in your vision. But you need to clarify exactly how your vision will deliver that service. It is one thing to say, "My vision will help people," but it is quite another to say "My vision will help to establish a healthy environment for latch-key children by opening an after-school youth club where they can enjoy free activities and tutoring." Your motivation will increase when you have defined and refined what your vision's service will be.

One danger here is to use the term "service" too narrowly. Some might interpret this purely in terms of "winning souls," or of helping the poor. They would contest that if the service doesn't achieve one of those objectives, then it is not a true service.

On the contrary, your service in the world, just like your vision, can look far different from anyone else's. If your vision is to spend your life as a researcher in a laboratory to better understand the composition of obscure particles, or as a physicist dealing with an abstract problem, you are providing a service by adding to humanity's body of knowledge. If your vision is to be an artist, you are providing a service through creative expression that enriches people's lives. And if your idea is to protect the environment you are providing a service to God's creation.

2. Does your vision redeem?
I would like to revisit the idea of redemptive vision. Put the question, "Does my vision redeem?" in the context of the first question, "Does my vision provide a service?" This gives some built-in boundaries.

It is not enough to provide a service. Gambling casinos and drug dealers provide a service, but these activities and many others are not redemptive. In fact, any occupation can become purely self-serving if redemptive values are marginalized. A doctor, a lawyer, a banker—anyone in any profession—can do their work just for the money and care less if that work adds any value to the world.

If your vision is going to redeem, you need to ask yourself: Does the vision point to God's reality? Does it reflect his character? Does it somehow better the world?

3. Is it really worth doing?
In *The Answer to How is Yes,* Peter Block reminds his readers that people have forgotten to ask the question of "how?" for themselves.[12]

To answer it, you need to determine what "worth" means to you. As you can imagine, worth is relative to everyone. It is formed by society's values, religious beliefs and personal philosophy.

Without going into a long philosophical discussion here, I simply propose that you start by considering how your vision matters to you as a person and then identify the value your vision will bring to God's kingdom. By reflecting on these two things you can gain a sense of the significance of your vision. Then you can answer, "Is it really worth it?"

4. Does your vision fit your gifting?
Do you truly understand your personal characteristics, interests, special skills and capabilities, what energizes you, and how you respond to a broken world?

If your vision involves a lot of social contact, yet you tend to be an introverted person, then you need to give careful consideration to whether the vision you have identified is one you want to pursue. If you embark on a journey that does not follow God's gifting in your life, you will end up being dissatisfied. As John Calvin put it, "You cannot know yourself unless you know God, and you cannot know God unless you know yourself."[13] What gifting has God put in your life, and does your vision fit into that?

5. Is your vision realistic?
A good vision is not an illusion. But for many people, that's all a vision is—a fantasy. You run from idea to idea with initial high hopes. Then you hit a barrier and bang—that dream is done and over, and you are on to a new venture. This pattern repeats because the image you tried to project on reality was in fact an unattainable illusion. Such cycles are evident when you jump from church to church, relationship to relationship, or job to job. You expect idealistic perfection but never find it. Or maybe you are consciously or unconsciously demanding perfection either in your vision or your ability to bring it to life. Fearing disappointment, you become discouraged and lose confidence, gradually giving up.

Eventually these patterns of unfulfilled idealism lead to cynicism. After each collapsed fantasy, you end up with disappointment and even despair. Yet you find yourself doing it again and again.

You need to ask yourself: is your vision one of these illusions? Is it just a flight of the imagination to a castle in the sky? Or is it a vision that can be grounded in reality and actually achieved?

6. What are your true motivations for pursuing this vision?
"Selfless" acts can make us feel good about ourselves, and sometimes "selfish" ones can benefit others. Get all of your motivations on the table at this point in the process and be unflinchingly honest with yourself. It is okay to do things for yourself, but your worldview is askew if these things take their incentive strictly from self-gratification. What are your *true* motivations for pursuing this vision?

What makes you come alive will likely make someone else come alive as well.

7. What are the relational implications?
Most visions have a social impact because they will impact relationships—family, friends, colleagues, etc. Some of these people may accept and support what you want to do while others will not. Your vision is also likely to open up relationships with new people. Ask yourself: what are the relational implications of my vision?

8. What are the economic implications?
God created an economic reality that is interwoven into this world. Everything has a financial link. Your vision, no matter what it is, possesses economic impact. In some cases those economic

implications will be small. In other cases they will be big enough that you might need to trim your vision back or even decide if it is worthwhile at all.

The economics of your vision may require you to leave your job, so you must consider where your funding will come from. Your vision may necessitate bringing others into the picture—how will they be supported?

In a later chapter we will deal with these issues in greater depth, but for now, address this question at its most basic level: what are the economic implications of your vision?

#

All of these questions establish a framework for evaluating the importance and worth of your vision. After a serious look at each of these criteria, you need to be confident that your vision has successfully filtered through them and has been distilled to a worthy pursuit you are confidant you can undertake.

Someone said you can over analyze things and thereby "achieve death by a thousand qualifications." That's not the purpose of these questions. They are there to give you a firm foundation as you move forward.

Questions:

5:1 Go back and answer each of the eight questions asked in this chapter. Carefully consider each one.

DAY 6
GOALS AND AGE GROUPS

You can retire from your career, but you will never retire from serving God. Rick Warren , The Purpose Driven Life

You worked hard in the last chapter. I'd like to take a break to address an area that may give you a bit of perspective. Vision applies to everyone, but everyone owns a different set of experiences through which they will build their vision. And those experiences vary depending on what age you are.

Under thirty
It might be difficult to realize a goal at seventy-three, but it's probably harder at twenty-three. When I ask students in their twenties, "what is your vision?", my answer is usually a blank stare. I propose a few reasons why.

There is the burden of pressures I mentioned earlier. Pressures to get an education, get a job, and to be what the immediate social system expects you to be. When you enter your twenties, you move beyond the academic routine of the education system and become more independent. Then all of a sudden you are faced with figuring out what you want to do with the rest of your life.

And the options are innumerable. If you choose one you can't have the others. And, if you choose one, what happens if it turns out to be the wrong choice? Stalemate.

Then there's the struggle with identity, which I won't even begin to address here (I recommend Dick Keyes' *Beyond Identity*). So if I ask this age group "what do you really want to do?" they often do not know themselves well enough to answer.

For anyone of any age — but especially for those still figuring out who they are — I'd advise against picking vision goals that are too grand for your present circumstances or are too idealistic. That can be a recipe for failure.

One twenty-four year old student named Stephen told me his vision of buying a huge piece of land near a metropolis. He wanted to build an artistic community where actors, writers, artists, and other "creatives" would come and work together. People from the nearby city would come and listen to readings, watch plays, etc. And the community would send evangelistic teams out around the world, and . . . . and . . . and . . .

Now that is all fine and wonderful, and perhaps some day

Stephen will see his vision realized. But he was still in the middle of his university studies with all the attached financial obligations. It is good to have big goals, but he would be better off by beginning with smaller steps. He could assist with or start an artistic program within an existing organization, or gather together artist friends informally on a regular basis, or some less over-extended version of his vision. That way he could allow his imagination to play in reality and see if he truly enjoyed the results.

I don't want to discourage anyone in this or any age group from pursuing big vision goals. I know another young man named Dimitri, twenty-three years old, who has a university degree in finance and accounting. He accepted a job in the financial department of a large, multinational company. While on a holiday to Romania, he saw many jobless people and a pressing need for economic development. He quit his job and moved to a remote Romanian city with one of the country's highest unemployment rates. There he found local partners from companies and universities and started a school of entrepreneurship. The first year's funding came from Dimitri's own pocket. He returned to his home country and raised money to fund the following three years. The school is expected to be internally funded by then.

Now, this is another big, idealistic goal for a young man who doesn't speak Romanian and has absolutely zero experience in founding a school. The difference between him and Stephan is that Dimitri woke up every day and took a concrete action toward his vision. He worked his way through the forest by putting one foot ahead of the other. He didn't waste time climbing all the trees (those "what if's" that didn't fit with his vision).

If you have a big vision, break it down into small actions that you can accomplish. My advice to vision-seekers in this age group is to try and find one thing that truly interests and excites you and that you can achieve in a short period of time. This may be linked to a longer-term goal, and accomplishing it will help you learn about yourself. With some experience under your belt, you can move forward to the larger visions. Take it one step at a time.

Thirty to fifty

In this age group, you often have enough life experience to be able to say, "this is who I am, this is what I feel is important, and this is what I want to do."

You also have a huge burden of responsibility, and to survive it you establish routines. Routines can be life-saving, but they can also be difficult to break. You start becoming part of the system rather than looking for positive ways to change it.

But being in the system can work to your advantage. It allows you to see opportunities for starting new ventures in your company, getting involved in ministries at your church, or initiating humanitarian projects.

To do these things, you need to be in charge of your routines instead of letting them be in charge of you. Carve out regular times away from your daily demands to think through the things you want to accomplish sooner and later.

I suggest identifying some small but significant short-term goal that fits on the continuum leading to that longer-term vision. If you are an architect who eventually wants to retire and lead architectural tours for Americans in Italy, you might start learning Italian or volunteer to give tours at your local museum. Take manageable actions toward what you ultimately desire to accomplish.

Fifty onwards

I'd like to set this up with two different examples of what the "retirement" age can do for you and others.

Couple Number One live on the west coast of the United States. He worked for the state government all his life and took early retirement. Almost every day, he plays golf with his wife near their home. They also travel to golf resorts in other states, especially Nevada. In Las Vegas, they play golf during the day and see the shows in the evening. They are Christians and they don't gamble. They have a boat on a lake, and a motorcycle for regular weekend road trips. They attend a very large church on Sunday where they enjoy "watching" the worship service with their retired golf friends. Conversation revolves around golf or where they went on their last trip and where they are going on their next one. They take a cruise ever year to Acapulco or Alaska. Welcome to "retirement."

Couple Number Two were both eighty years old. They lived about twenty miles outside of Geneva, Switzerland. Geneva is an international city where thousands of English-speaking people work, and many of them commute to satellite villages nearby. This couple walked through those villages frequently. They began to notice the names on the mailboxes, many of which were not Swiss. Then they asked each other, "Where do these people go to church?" Geneva was a bit too far away, and there were no English-speaking churches in the area. They prayed about it and gathered together a small group of families who shared their vision to start a church. Since then this couple has passed away, but today their church is thriving and alive, meeting a real need in that area.

Now, I have nothing against golf or other recreational activities, but I have serious questions as to whether Couple Number One is doing something meaningful with their lives. I recently saw a television special about the condition of the educational system in the city where they live. High school students were asking the interviewer, "why do other schools get books and teachers and we don't?"

Granted, Couple Number One may not have interests or passions linked to education. If not, they could find an area of need in their community or church that did interest them and assist there. They have the time and resources to share and demonstrate God's love in any number of capacities. But if they continue to be oblivious to the needs around them, they could well just play golf until they die.

Couple Number Two was fulfilling their general, God-given job description to tend to and redeem the world around them through the distinct job of starting a church. If our basic job description is to tend the world around us and redeem it, then that is not something that stops when we become sixty-five. This is actually a time of life when many of us have good health, financial security and a wealth of knowledge and experience to bring to the world. We can certainly slow down and have some fun, but let's be careful of thinking that's all we are called to do.

I advise this age group to purposely look for needs around them. And then meet these needs. Find something that interests you. You have knowledge, experience and some capital to make a difference.

Don't just live for your own pleasure. Instead, think in terms of *the one last important thing I can do to make the world better*? What is it? This is your last chance.

#

At every age, consider: a) an understanding of the needs in your own life, b) an understanding of the needs in the world, and c) your response to these needs.

Questions:

6:1 What are the needs and desires in your own life and how do you respond to them? Your needs might be personal aspirations, emotional healing, spiritual development, or generally betterment.

6:2 How do you perceive the needs and desires in the world and how do you respond to them?

DAY 7
YOUR STORY

Vision – it reaches beyond the thing that is, into the conception of what can be. Imagination gives you the picture. Vision gives you the impulse to make the picture your own. Robert Collier, *Writer, Publisher*

At this point, you have hopefully identified your vision and determined that it is valuable and worth pursuing. Now you make it happen. To do that, it helps to see your new adventure in the context of a narrative: a story. If you understand the key components of narrative, you will be better prepared for some of the dynamics you will encounter.

#

The journey of bringing your vision to life is an adventure. Some day you will be able to look back at the entire process and share it with others by saying, "Here is my story."

Your journey is an adventure story

This is basic stuff, but perhaps you haven't thought of the vision builder in terms of narrative before. When you begin to read a story, you usually find a main character, the protagonist, within a particular setting or situation. Something happens that launches that hero or heroine on a quest to reach a goal, whether physical, emotional or spiritual.

This is the timeless setup: "Once upon a time something happened." Take the protagonist Frodo the Hobbit in *The Lord of The Rings*.[14] Frodo lives a normal Hobbit life in his idyllic little village until one day something happens. A wizard comes along and gives him a ring to take to a far away place and destroy. Thus Frodo begins his quest.

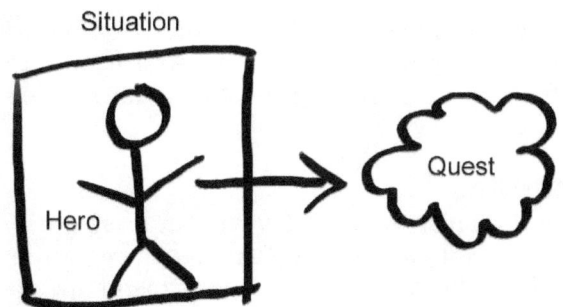

Or a retired spy is blamed for a crime he didn't do and then goes on a quest to clear his name. Or a woman meets a man and then goes on a quest to win his love—and vice versa. There are endless variations on this theme, and the formula can be found most everywhere. Why? Because that's how things tend to be—your vision-building endeavor included.

You find yourself in a situation (your life at this moment), something happens (you discover a vision), and voila, "Once upon a time" is underway. Now you have the choice, like all the characters I mentioned above, 'to action out' of your situation and start the quest to achieve your vision

The question is, are you really going to take that action? Risk is involved for Frodo, the retired spy and the woman. Many people stay in their current situation because they are afraid of the risk. Are you going to remain in fear or step out into the unknown?

Stepping into the unknown forest

Stories are adventures, even the ones where no big-budget "action" is happening. Stories start by stepping into the proverbial forest. It is not coincidental that many of Grimm's fairy tales take place in a forest. The dense, dark wooded space is an illustration of the unknown. You come to the edge of a thick forest, and you can't see where the path will take you.

But that is how your story begins. If you truly feel passionate about your vision, you will step into the forest. Like the protagonists in most good stories, you have something serious at stake—your vision.

The thing about your vision is that often it's outside of yourself. It's something that you've never done before. And in almost all cases, it exists outside your normal, probably comfortable, life patterns.

Know your enemies

When you have a protagonist, you usually have at least one antagonist as well. The 'bad guy.' But he/she/it can be harder to identify in a vision quest, because your antagonist isn't always a person. It could be a concept, a fear, or even a destructive pattern in the main character's mind.

Know that your antagonist will try to stop you from achieving your quest. Therefore it is important that you know the enemies in your life. I have often had to deal with this. Because of my business relationships, I receive an inordinate number of demands to look at new ideas and opportunities and to spend time with people reviewing their business plans. These encounters are usually unproductive and eat up my time—valuable time I need to pursue my vision. Over the last few years I have had to consciously cut back on business engagements in order to devote more time to my passions, one of which is writing this book to help you live *your* passion.

Character development

Following your passion will present you with many challenges. How you respond to those challenges will enable you to learn, to grow and mature: character development. If Frodo had not learned anything on his journey, *The Lord of the Rings* would have been a flat story. Thankfully, J. R. R. Tolkein knew how intrinsic character development is to a narrative.

Most of you can look back at a rough experience in your past and see that you grew and learned despite the difficulty or even pain involved. So hang in there when things get hard. When a fisherman repairs a damaged net, the spot he reinforces is stronger and more resilient than parts that were never damaged.

#

Remember that this story is your individual adventure. You get to decide whether to step into the forest, whether to know and prepare for your enemies once inside, and whether to face challenges or give in to fear.

Once upon a time . . . .

Questions:

7:1 What or who are your enemies that will stop you from achieving your vision? In an earlier chapter, you examined what was stopping you from achieving your vision. Revisit this and see if anything else has occurred to you. It is important to know your enemies so that you can answer the next question.

7:2 How are you going to deal with your enemies? Now that you know your enemies, how are you doing to conquer them? Do you have any "combat" strategies in place? If not, develop a battle plan here.

DAY 8
VISION AND FAITH

Faith has to do with things that are not seen, and hope with things that are not in hand.   Saint Thomas Aquinas

There are two ways to enter the forest. Either you step forward entirely on your own, or you engage God in your endeavor. I don't know about you, but I don't want to find myself alone in the dark against unseen enemies.

Are you on your own?
If you are, you are managing your vision quest through a materialist's perspective. The materialist paradigm essentially says that the material is all there is. Therefore, if I want to achieve anything in this world, I need to learn techniques to manipulate the material reality. For instance, if I want to go somewhere in a car, I need to learn how to drive the car. If I want to run a company, I need to learn all the right management techniques. Fair enough. But of course, it's not as simple as that.

As Francis Schaeffer explained in *The God Who Is There*, if you are a materialist, you see the world as a 'closed system'.[15] What you see is all there is. When you attempt to achieve a vision, you do so from your own resources, starting from and depending purely on yourself.

This view may initially seem attractive. Ah to be the rugged, individual hero facing challenges solo. Maybe in theory. Maybe. Personally I'd rather have a helping hand if I find myself standing face to face with a dragon on my adventure.

Even if you feel exceptionally heroic, if you are a materialist, you are operating from an incomplete view of reality. Reality is made up of more than what we can just see, touch and manipulate.

The unseen reality
Anglo-Irish satirist Jonathan Swift said that "Vision is the art of seeing things invisible." Indeed, reality consists of both the seen and the unseen: an "open system." An open system allows for interaction between the spiritual world and the physical world. This allows you to see both the process of realizing your vision and the process of achieving your vision within a much broader framework than the materialist.

Francis Schaeffer also said, "Real history involves both the seen and the unseen, often in a cause and effect relationship . . . We must remember that we are creatures in the total reality of history."[16]

Within the open system you find a multitude of spiritualities. But the Christian view is quite different from all the rest. It starts from the position of a loving, faithful and all-powerful God who has created the heavens and the earth, who exists and is present in his creation. Because of the original fall in the Garden of Eden and each person's failure to achieve God's perfection and holiness, humans were separated from him.

God offers a solution to that separation: his Son. Christ is the one and only mediator between humans and God. Through the working of the Holy Spirit in our lives and by accepting what God has done for us, we can become spiritually redeemed. And that redemption can work its way out into redeeming the brokenness of all the areas of the world around us.

#

The Christian also holds that God is engaged in his creation. That fact directly relates to your vision and your pursuit of it, because God is the one who provides you with the visionary idea, and he walks with you through the journey of achieving it. He provides you with courage and insight as you step into the unknown forest. He is the one I want with me when I face each "dragon."

Not all visions come from God. This is a broken world with fallen people who can have broken visions. Adolph Hitler is one of the quintessential examples of a visionary whose vision was terribly wrong. He is a worst-case scenario example, but don't let pride convince you that you can't be misguided on a far smaller, much subtler scale.

Test your vision out with God. Pray, meditate on his word, and seek wise council. The following diagram shows how God is the covering for your vision as a vision-building story. He is engaged from beginning to end:

Engage the Lord
Nehemiah of the Old Testament understood this. He held a trustworthy position reporting directly to the king of a vast empire. One day, he met some of his fellow Jews coming from Jerusalem. When Nehemiah asked them how things were there, he learned that Jerusalem's situation was grim. That news greatly disturbed him.

But he did not leap into action to solve Jerusalem's problems. His first response was to take his concerns to God. Nehemiah prayed for several months. One day the king finally noticed Nehemiah's sadness and inquired about the cause. At that point, Nehemiah shared his burden while silently asking God for courage.

Nehemiah asked the king if he could return to Jerusalem to rebuild the city of his fathers. The king agreed. Only then did Nehemiah begin the long journey to his wounded city in need.

His initial vision was basically a construction project, to rebuild Jerusalem's broken walls. Once he accomplished that, he moved on to another phase, which was to restore the broken society in Judah. It wasn't easy. Nehemiah's enemies tried to stop him, so he not only had to rebuild the walls; he had to protect them as the work was being done.

Notice that Nehemiah engaged God at all points in his project, from beginning to end. He acted within the reality of an open system with a cause-and-effect relationship between the seen and the unseen. His faith was evident in each phase of formulating and pursuing his vision.

Unfortunately many Christians operate from a dual reality. On Sunday they go to church, pray and worship God. The rest of the week—or even as soon as the car pulls out of the church parking lot—they act as materialists in a closed system, doing everything on their own strength as though the spiritual world were nonexistent. The more consistent Biblical perspective is that God is involved *at all times.* He isn't just with you on Sunday mornings.

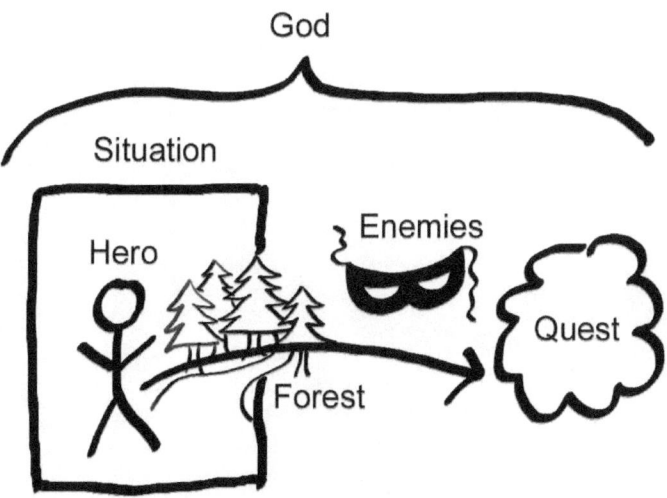

If you believe in a spiritual world, then you recognize that God is involved in your current situation. You understand that he has placed a vision in your heart and given you the competency to bring it to life. You know that he will enter with you into the unknown forest and will empower you to face your enemies. And you know, even as hard as it can be, that he will use these circumstances to develop your character.

This is the life of faith: trusting God and engaging him at every action of the journey.

Question:

8:1 How does your vision fit into your spirituality? How is God involved in the origin and initiation of your vision idea? How will you engage with God as you go on your vision-building journey, facing the unknowns in the forest and confronting your enemies?

DAY 9
REFRAMING YOUR VISION

A vision is something you see and others don't.
Anita Roddick, *Founder of The Body Shop*

With the foundational concepts in the last few chapters in your mind, revisit your vision statement. Anything to tweak, change, overhaul?

If your vision doesn't inspire you, you won't be inspired to bring it to life

Remember that your vision statement is not a plan. It is where you want to go. Your quest. If your written statement sounds flat, rewrite it until it takes on a special meaning to you and you can't wait to make it happen.

I once consulted with a European business unit within a large, multinational electronics company. It was by far the fastest growing unit in the company, and they made a considerable profit contribution. The managers of that unit had a vision statement. It was: "Nobody owes us a Living."

That probably means nothing to you and me, but it meant everything to them. Until they joined this business unit, most of its managers were underachievers on the verge of being asked to resign. Then they banded together, drafted their vision statement, got motivated, and collectively started achieving a screaming success. The rest of the corporation didn't understand them or that statement. That was irrelevant to them. Unlike the rest of the business units in this company who held their management meetings in stuffy conference rooms, these managers could be found windsurfing on the Mediterranean, hang gliding in the Alps and canoeing crocodile-infested rivers in Africa.

Before choosing "Nobody owes us a Living" for their vision statement, this unit had been funded by other businesses within the company. They got the equivalent of hand-outs from units who looked down on them. But armed with their new vision, this unit began to run a self-sufficient and profitable business.

For these formerly floundering managers, a universe of meaning and values was imbedded in their one simple vision statement. So don't worry if other people don't understand or relate to yours.

The important thing is that it means something to you and that it inspires you.

Nuts and bolts
Your vision statement will typically be a short phrase that may contain any or all of the following components:

It isn't status quo: Your vision differs from what currently exists. It is a quest for something new. Things are going to change if you bring it to life.

It is future-oriented: Because your vision will be something new, it is future-oriented. That means that it contains a picture—either explicitly or implicitly—of how things will be in the future. Your vision statement may or may not include a sense of timing.

It matters: Doing what matters revs your motivation dramatically. Your vision should capture the potential of a better, redeemed reality on a spiritual, social, economic, or ecological level.

It is active: Your vision should contain a sense of movement. Think of verbs like: grow, change, provide, bring, lead. These express action and transformation.

It is based on a fundamental belief: Your beliefs will and should pervade all areas of your life, especially your vision.

Essentially, your vision statement should express the destination you are headed in a way that builds your commitment. Some examples from students of mine:

My vision is to express and live off my artistic capabilities and to see people be encouraged through my art.

My vision is to have a new living situation where I can bring up my family in a more constructive environment.

My vision is to run my own successful architecture company specializing in redesigning and renovating old industrial sites.

My vision is to have a company that creates software programs that will enable people to make better use of their time.

My vision is to improve the financial situation of some of the poorest women in India by starting micro-loan operations this year.

My vision is to change lives in the inner city, spiritually, socially, and economically by being a spiritual role model while tutoring high school students from poor families, enabling them to get jobs and go to university.

These vision statements may not mean much to you, but they hold tremendous meaning to their authors. Each visionary sees the needs in the world around them differently and responds with their individual interests and competencies.

Some of these statements are vague while others provide direction by describing a changed state in the future. It is even better if you leave it general. Don't worry; the next actions will give you some specifics on how to get there.

Question:

9:1 Using some or all of the components listed above, rewrite your vision in a way that captures both the importance of what you are doing and the passion you feel for it. Keep it to around fifty words or less.

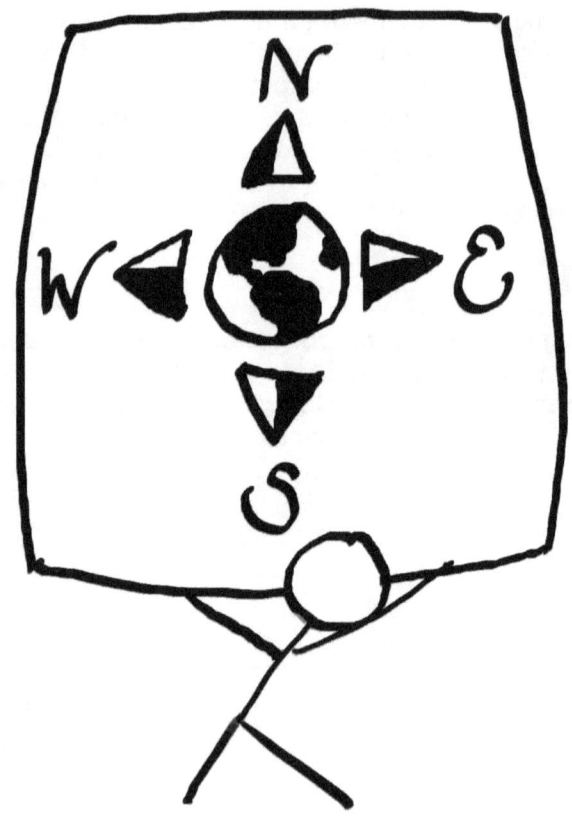

Action Two
Establish your Map

DAY 10
THE CARTOGRAPHER

It's not how many ideas you have.
It's how many ideas you make happen.
From a television commercial

You are the cartographer. You draw your own map for this journey. To make your idea happen, you have to allocate time and resources to laying it out. Your vision won't happen unless you make it happen.

That means you need a strategy. In his book *Strategy Safari*, Henry Mintzberg identifies ten different schools of strategy, including the Design School, the Cognitive School, the Learning School, the Configuration School, etc.[17] Each of these schools approaches strategy differently, and you could spend an entire university semester course studying one. Thankfully Mintzberg simplifies everything by compacting strategy into two general types: strategy as a forward-looking plan and strategy as internal patterns.

Strategy as a forward-looking plan
With this strategy, you look into the future and build targets, actions, and dates into a cohesive structure. This is how most people use the word "strategy."

For companies, "strategy as a forward-looking plan," usually involves looking at a current situation, seeing what most needs to be done, and then developing methods for achieving those objectives. At this point, the planners will set key priorities, milestones, and allocation of responsibilities. Then this cascades down through the organization so that everyone knows what to do to support the plan.

The details of this strategic planning may sound familiar or not, but they are essential to following through with your vision. As is Mintzberg's second strategy.

Strategy as internal patterns
Whether or not your vision comes to life is intricately knotted to your existing patterns of behavior. "Strategy as internal patterns" involves knowing what patterns work for you and changing the ones that don't. As you know, changing internal patterns can be extremely difficult. Say your New Year's resolutions were to lose

weight and keep your office in order. Four months later your weight is the same and you could hide a month's supply of Girl Scout cookies under the towering piles of paper on your desk.

What happened here? Nothing changed in your life. You continued with the same patterns of behavior. To change (to achieve your objectives), you have to change patterns in your life.

If you have a problem making time for new projects, ask yourself what unnecessary activities can be time-limited, or even eliminated entirely. The average retired American spends 40 hours a week sitting in front of the television. Forty hours. That's a full time job. While you may only watch the occasional news or show in the evenings, you will still be surprised if you do the following. Keep a TV log for a week or two, without skipping any of your normal shows. Just write down how much TV you watch each day, average your hours and see how much of the day you could be spending doing anything else (like pursuing a vision). Change your existing pattern. If you don't, you are unlikely to bring your vision to life.

#

I knew a man with a vision to help students in the inner city. He had a passion for his vision and knew it would fill a great need. He had a degree in sociology but his current job was in administration. He enjoyed his job and wanted to do the inner-city work in his spare time.

The problem was, he didn't have any spare time. All of his out-of-office time was swallowed up with church activities. He taught a Sunday school class, sang in the choir, attended weekly meetings, social meetings, special events, planning meetings, dinners with church friends and so on. Certainly church participation is necessary and wonderful, but God's Church extends beyond the walls of a sanctuary and includes those children in the city he so desired to help.

Learning to say no and setting priorities are difficult processes. You have to make hard choices. People on vision quests are focused and single-minded. When you are truly passionate about a vision, you minimize activities that don't contribute. You make constant choices to focus on the path that will lead toward your goal. If you deviate into non-vision activities, you are quick to realize it and immediately take corrective action to redirect yourself.

Getting rid of disruptive and irrelevant patterns can be dramatic and difficult. It might mean having to leave your job for one that is less time consuming. It might mean bowing out from dinner invitations or clubs or other social activities. It certainly means less time watching television and wiling away hours at the shopping mall.

One woman I know found herself watching too much television years ago. She gave up all TV for a year and now has no desire to watch it. She even gave away her TV and had time to write a book.

#

What are you going to change? If you know this, you will be able to establish your roadmap.

Questions:

10:1 What patterns of behavior and routines will stop you from achieving your vision?

10:2 How are you going to deal with them?

DAY 11
THE LEGEND – YOUR PLAN

Planning is nothing. Plans are everything
Traditional business wisdom

As you saw in the last chapter, you need strategy to manage the patterns of behavior in your life. Now you turn to drafting a strategic plan, the other essential aspect of strategy.

If you were attending a school of entrepreneurship at a university, you would be taught to put together intricate business plans. These can exceed one hundred pages once you add the appendices, and preparing them can be an extremely time-consuming exercise. I've seen entrepreneurs spend many months working on their plan when they should have been working on their project.

Instead of sending you off to draft pages of plans, I want to guide you through a couple of things you need to consider and to introduce you to the questions you will be answering for your vision.

Be flexible

None of the tactics in your plan are set in stone. Prussian field marshal Helmuth von Moltke wisely noted that, "No plan survives contact with reality." The same holds with your visionary plan, so remind yourself that no visionary plan survives contact with reality either. As any military leader knows, you enter the battle with both a set of tactics and the understanding that those tactics will have to be flexible to survive the unknown realities on the battle field.

Likewise, most business leaders make both tactical plans and contingency or scenario plans. A contingency plan considers flexible approaches for achieving their tactical plan. This planner will ask questions like: "what if the economy remains the same, or dramatically improves, or gets worse? How will this impact my plan?" While military leaders and business leaders will start their engagement with a set tactical plan, they remain open to contingencies that might impact the plan.

So establish your tactics, but remember that once you enter the unknown forest you need to be prepared to make modifications. You never know what might cross your path.

Definition creep

You have a vision to become a full-time artist. A painter. So you decide you'll buy a house with a large studio that gets good light for oil painting and maybe ceramics (you saw a potters' wheel for sale in the classifieds). That means you need an adjoining room for your computer to do graphic design to support the painting, because all the mess from the clay and glaze isn't good for technical equipment. And since you've got the computer there, why not help your friend write her children's books? You can illustrate them. And you have always dreamt of having a bed and breakfast. But really, it would be easy to make the house an artistic salon where artists can come from near and far to show and critique their work. And not just artists, because you just heard about the most amazing center that blends art with political activism, and you want to be a citizen who makes a difference, so maybe you should add . . . .

Um, what happened to the full-time painter?

One large danger in planning is called 'definition creep.' This is when you start piling more and more details or functionality onto your basic definition, your vision statement. It starts with saying, "Wouldn't it be great if we added this? Oh, and let's add this. And wouldn't this also be nice?" You start gluing on so many bells and whistles that the vision isn't even visible anymore.

Definition creep can happen at the beginning of a project, and it can happen after you are well under way. In all cases, stay away from definition creep. I advise keeping your vision to one clear concept and keeping your plans simple and extremely focused on that one concept. Definition creep can kill the project.

Be flexible and keep it simple.

Factors to establish your map

In the following chapters, you will be answering these questions in light of your vision:[18]

1. Domain—Who and What? What is the 'product' of your vision? Who is the recipient of your vision—who is your audience, consumer, or participant? What is the lay of the land?

2. Compass—Where? Where will your vision be produced (brought to life) and how will you get it to your recipients?

3. Tools and choosing them—How? How will you get organized? What does your workspace look like, what tools will you use, and how will you make decisions?

Depending on your vision, one of these questions may be more important than another, but carefully consider them all. I elaborate on each question in the following chapters. When you write your answers, you have begun to face the very real task of implementing your vision. The next actions will require stepping into the forest, into the unknown. As you move forward, you will find out just how important your vision is to you.

A warning: your vision may start to look so enormous that you begin to feel threatened by it. If you fall back into habitual patterns of negative thinking, you may find yourself saying "I can't do this. It is too big." Don't let this happen. Keep your dream in your mind at all times. Do you really want it? If you do, you'll stay motivated because you will be acting from your visionary passion.

And also remember that your greatest resource and strength will not come from yourself but the almighty God who loves you and supports you. He gave you your vision, and he will be with you as you work to make it happen.

After answering these chapter questions, you are ready to move on to the questions for your plan in the following chapters. As you do, remember to imagine, innovate, and create.

Questions:

11:1 Keeping flexible planning in mind, write out what might happen if your vision is a huge success, a static endeavor, or a huge failure. What are your plans in each scenario?

11:2 Examine your tendencies for expanding definitions in your life. Have you already started to let extraneous elements creep into your plans? What can you do to remind yourself of your specific vision?

DAY 12
DOMAIN – WHO AND WHAT?

What is the 'product' of your vision? Who is the recipient of your vision – who is your audience, consumer, or participant? What is the lay of the land?

Call it the businessman's approach. I want to help you see your vision in the context of some business models for establishing your map.

The previous chapter gave you a "legend" for that map, and the first factor addressed domain. Domain encompasses the product or service you will provide and the people who will be using it (recipients). It also encompasses communication with your recipients and understanding the lay of the land – the environment where your vision will be happening.

Every vision, if implemented, will eventually work its way out into something specific, and there will be someone who will be impacted by it. Some serious work is needed, but you need to precisely define this.

What is the product of your vision?

Every vision has a product or service embedded within it. That 'product' is a specific thing or service that will benefit your recipients. Ask yourself of your vision, "What is my product and exactly who will be using it?" Keep in mind that the word 'product' applies even if you are not creating a tangible good. When I use 'product' I am also implying service.

Your product is different from your vision, yet it supports the achievement of your vision. If your vision is to help young, unwed mothers, your product may be counseling services and job placement. Or your product may be a day-care center that looks out for the children while the mothers work. Or your product may be the establishment of a training program on child care. Each of these 'products' is different, yet they all support the same vision. You need to decide and define exactly what product will support your vision.

If your dream is to start your own company, define exactly what products and services you will be offering. If your dream is to go back to university, decide on your major and even the electives you will take, as well as specifically define how you will use that education once you are finished. If your dream is to mend broken relationships in your family, identify the precise 'service' or process you will use to bring those relationships back together.

Product is different than outcome. An electronics company might have computers as its product. The outcome is both the revenue from the sale of those computers and the satisfied customers who buy them.

Outcome applies outside the business world, too. If your vision is to be a writer, think about what you want to write: fiction, nonfiction, poetry? The outcome might be publication and engaged readers who gain something from your writing. Get specific when defining what your vision provides.

Your vision statement must be backed up with a precisely defined product and outcome; otherwise your vision will remain vague and so will you.

Who are the recipients of your vision?

Besides yourself, who will benefit from your vision? And where will they benefit from it?

If you plan to provide consulting services, not only do you have to answer the question of exactly what those services are (your product) but also who your recipients are — who will be using your product? Large or small companies? In what business sector?

Maybe your vision involves changing your profession. In this case, your recipient is yourself, but there are likely to be others who will benefit from your new occupation. Who are they?

Someone else will always benefit from your vision. If you are starting a non-profit organization, who exactly are your recipients? Can you describe them by demographics? What are the economic and other critical factors in the environment in which you will operate?

By understanding this information, you will be prepared to make good decisions while implementing your plan. You will know where to focus your efforts.

If you incorrectly define your target recipients, then you will be wasting time. The more knowledge you have about them, the more likely you are to succeed.

What is your communication plan?

In almost all cases, people will be impacted by your vision. If you are producing a product or service, you need to inform your market about it and to explain its benefits. How will you communicate with those potential recipients? How will you make them aware of the product offering or the change resulting from your vision? The answer: with a communication plan.

For instance, if your vision is to start a branch of Mothers of Preschoolers in your church, then you need to work out how you are going to approach the church leaders and then how you will 'advertise' to your recipients—mothers who would benefit from using the program.

The lay of the land

Do some research and find out if someone else is offering similar products or services. If so, you will face competition and may be vying for the same resources. Or you could join forces with the competition and become partners as you find ways to work together. You need to compare the relative strengths and weakness of your own offering, which in turn will help you identify niche areas where you will succeed in achieving your vision. Be aware of your position in relation to others who are doing similar things.

#

The product of my vision is this book. You, as the reader and user of this book, are my recipient. I happen to communicate directly with you through this, my product. Other authors have addressed vision—and I'm thankful for their works—but my niche is my entrepreneurial and business background in a spiritual context.

See how it works?

Questions:

12:1 What's your product?

12:2 Who's your recipient, and in what environment will they be receiving your product?

12:3 What is your plan for communicating with the people engaged in your vision and/or those who will use your product or service?

12:4 Who else is doing the same thing and how does that impact you?

DAY 13
COMPASS – WHERE?

Where will your vision be produced (brought to life) and how will you get it to your recipients?

Your vision will remain in the realm of your imagination until it becomes grounded in reality. Where will your vision be happening? Your basement, church, an office, a foreign country? How will the benefactors of the vision be receiving it? By mail, delivery, in a classroom, over the radio?

Where will you produce your product?
If your vision is to start an environmental awareness newsletter, you might start in a basement—your basement? A friend's? If it grows, where will it move? To an office building? Where?

Be as specific as you can. Ideally, you should be able to name the area of town where your vision is going to be produced. You might even have an address or two in mind or be able to draw the layout for a facility as yet unbuilt.

A student in one of my courses found it difficult to fit her vision into this question. She was a gifted writer, and that was her passion. I encouraged her to think about what she would be writing and where she would do her best writing. While some writers function best writing late at night from their spare room, others function better at a bustling cafe in broad daylight. This woman's ideal place turned out to be a small house surrounded by nature and a body of water. In the paper she submitted, she was able to describe this beautifully and in quite some detail.

This question begins to ground your vision. It brings it to reality, into physical bricks and mortar.

How will you produce it?
There are a myriad of ways to do things. Your production process may simply be you working on your own personal computer at home. Or your production process may involve the delegation of duties to a staff in a building designated for the use of distributing your vision product.

If you have a commercial venture, you will probably need to work with suppliers, and when it comes to manufacturing your product you may not want to do everything on your own. Therefore you may want to outsource certain aspects of the production.

When you begin to think about the production of your product, remember that there is always more than one way. Think about your different alternatives. Don't immediately lock yourself into one method, but also don't keep your options open indefinitely. Start with one mode of production and work from there.

How will you get it to your recipients?

Once your product is ready, ask yourself how you will supply it to your recipients. This is distribution. In the case of a service, determine how to make it available. Will you meet with people face-to-face or will you have intermediaries who deliver your service? In the case of a physical product, how will you distribute it to your recipients?

Questions:

13:1 Where will you produce your vision's product?

13:1 How will you produce it?

13:3 How will you deliver it to your recipients?

DAY 14
TOOLS AND CHOOSING THEM – HOW?

How will you get organized? What does your workspace look like, what tools will you use, and how will you make decisions?

In dry terms, this is the organizational and administrative part of your vision. The stuff you wish someone else could do for you but which you try to make more fun by going to a big office supply store to buy new pens, file tabs, day planners and . . . .

But pencil and paper work just fine. Ask yourself:

1. **What's your vision's structure?**
2. **What kind of resources do you need and when?**
3. **How many, if any, staff will you need in the near and far future?**
4. **What kind of network of people will you need (familial support can fall into this category too)**
5. **Who are your key contacts? (Translation: who do you know?)**
6. **What associations should you join now?**
7. **What educational institutions should you link up with?**
8. **What kind of support system do/will you have outside my own organization? (This can be as basic as Grandma watching the kids a few times a week while you work on your vision.)**
9. **What's your legal structure?**

Ah, we should pause here for a moment.

Legal structure?
"But my vision is to quit my job and be with my family full-time. Why do I need a legal structure?" you may ask. Maybe you only

need to devise a budget and do some basic financial planning. But many visions, commercial or not, will involve the creation of some kind of organization. If so, then early in the process, decide how you want to be legally structured. Will your vision end up a one-person show, a partnership, an association, or something that involves shareholders?

A four-woman stand-up improv group performs seasonally for fun. Each member has her own daytime job. But when they first came together, they understood that they should set up a separate business account. That allows them to cash checks in their group's name and divvy up even the modest revenue they generate without placing the burden of finances and taxes on one of the members.

If you are going to raise support for your activities, or if clients pay for your services, then you need to open a bank account and specify the account holder. Is the account in your name as an individual, or in the name of a legal entity, like that of the *improv* group?

Partners, investors, shareholders

Whether your husband or wife is going to watch the kids while you teach a cooking class at church or is going to help you start a bakery, he or she is your partner. Obviously, starting a legal business will require different amounts of paperwork than will the weekly babysitting, but both should be laid out clearly.

Get everybody's expectations out on the table. Choose people you know you can work well with (friends sometimes make terrible business partners). Write down—don't just discuss—what kind of work the participants will be doing, and in what capacity you will work together. Don't forget to address how people will be remunerated, whether it be that you cook your spouse a special dinner for two every Friday or you split the bakery profits with your business partner fifty-fifty.

Whatever you do, don't begin the arrangement with a vague agreement. If you do, expectations will shift constantly as they hit the reality of your project. This opens the door for conflict. You'll have enough obstacles to face without that. Sit down with those involved, pray for God's guidance in the discussion, and get it on paper.

Getting everybody organized

If other people are working with you to achieve your vision, get organized. Decide who is accountable to whom (a reminder: put God at the top of this list). Then discuss with the appropriate people:

Who will make decisions?

1. How you will work together with decision makers to your best advantage in terms of time and effort?
2. What activities should your vision avoid?

And whoever gets to crunch numbers . . .

Do you need to keep records?

1. Keep track of inventories, orders, shipments?
2. Will you keep records in a notebook or will you require computer software or an accountant to handle these?
3. How will you keep track of monies paid into your account?

If you are achieving your vision on your own, then you will likely be making all the decisions. If you have engaged other people in your endeavor, then decision-making becomes more complex.

Questions:

14:1 Go back and answer all the questions in this chapter. This may take some time but it is important that you answer each one of them. This lays the foundation for your entrepreneurial endeavor. It is the first step in knowing what infrastructure you will need to achieve your idea.

DAY 15
THERE IS A BOTTOM LINE

When I chased after money, I never had enough. When I got my life on purpose and focused on giving of myself to everything that arrived into my life, then I was prosperous. Wayne Dyer, *Psychotherapist*

Let's step aside for a moment and think about money in a spiritual context. Money is everywhere. You can't escape it, especially when you are bringing a vision to life. It is important to acknowledge that there is a financial reality. The bottom line is: there is a bottom line.

Yes, your vision has economics . . .
Think carefully through the financial resources you need, where you will find them and how you will spend them. I've watched many visions go astray because of poor financial understanding and neglectful management of economic realities. This is often the case in the Christian world, where views and attitudes towards money can get rather peculiar. Do any of these sound familiar?

View #1: Bankrolling God
I've met quite a few Christian vision builders who have told me that they are carrying out their project to make "tons of money" to give away to Christian works.

There is nothing wrong in giving money away to Christian works. In fact, the Bible has many references that command believers to support widows and orphans and to help the poor. The problem here is the focus on making 'tons' of money. This can defocus the vision builder from effectively managing the visionary process. The vision loses importance while the money-making gains importance – even becoming the new focus.

Why does this happen? One reason is the age-old love of money. Another is the desire to gain the power perceived to be attached to wealth. And yet another is a fear-based need to gain recognition from other people.

Christians may also fall for the worldview that proclaims spiritual ideals to be more important than the physical world. This view originates from Greek philosophy wherein the world of ideals held greater value than the tangible, physical world. The latter was seen as a lower order whose primary purpose was to serve the higher, spiritual order.

At its most basic level, this view looks something like this:

**Higher Level Spiritual World
("Christian" works)**

**Lower Level Material World
(social, political, ecological and economic works)**

Because of this belief, some Christian vision builders decide that their project is just an instrument to make money. They say this will free them to support those other, "higher" things that are more noble and good. The problem is that if making money is your primary motivation for pursuing a vision, you will have a greater tendency to devalue your vision and focus on dollar signs.

View #2: I scratch God's back, God scratches mine

Another view I've seen with Christian vision builders is what I call 'The Reward Model' which says "If I do something of value to God, then God will financially reward me." This attitude shifts your emphasis away from wisely managing a project for its own value to doing it only because you await God's financial reward. God is not a puppet.

This attitude might say such things as, "If I walk in the spirit then God will bless me financially." Or: "If I support social causes, or start a new company, or am absolutely holy, or if I evangelize . . . then I will receive a financial reward."

Besides being a weak theology, this view robs your vision of its inherent importance as a creative and redeeming action in the world. That importance itself—God-given as it is—should be where your passion for the vision quest originates. Not from the "reward money" you have decided God will give you.

View #3: 'Faithalistic' finances

The 'faithalistic' view is fatalism disguised as faith. The logic behind it goes something like this: "No matter what I do, God will provide." Yes, in the Bible you can see that God is the great provider. Yes he is there and he supports his people. But he also expects you to do your share of "tending to" things. God is God and generally it seems he does not expect you to passively sit back and wait for manna from heaven. Doing so is telling God what he will do for you—the wrong attitude to base your actions (or inaction) upon.

Even the Children of Israel had to fulfill their daily responsibilities as God regularly provided their daily nourishment.

This faithlistic attitude leads you to do your job in a sloppy fashion because, "God will cover for me." This affects your attitude about how money is managed. It says "I don't have to pay attention to all that, because God can pick up my slack with miracles." This produces inattentiveness to, and even mismanagement of, your funds.

If you go out into the woods for an indefinite time, you are wise to pack the necessary provisions and have faith that God will be with you along the path. And yes, if necessary, he can provide manna. But on his terms, not yours.

Don't get me wrong. We should live lives of faith and dependence on God no matter what our life activities, but faith should never be used as a cover for laziness, sloppiness, and wasteful living.

With some people and in some organizations, the faithalistic worldview is often an excuse for poor management and ends up wasting resources. It has similarities with the sluggard who desires and ends up having nothing.

Are you going to choose fatalism or faith?

The economic reality: get your foundation solid

The preceding views toward money fail because we live in an economic reality along with a spiritual, ecological, social reality, etc. You can see this economic reality via these foundational principles:

1. Spirituality is an earthly reality

The spiritual world is not separate from the physical world. In his book '*On the Way*' Gordon Smith writes: "Spirituality encompasses the whole of life . . . True spirituality is not otherworldly; rather, it enables us to be fully in the world."[19] Spirituality is not exclusive to so-called 'spiritual' things like prayer or mission work. Every part of our earthly reality involves spirituality, including the economic part.

This is not a pantheistic concept that says that 'all is God.' It is saying that the infinite, personal God is concerned with and engaged in every area of reality, both the seen and the unseen. Our task is to bring his lordship into every area of reality and not just relegate it to church on Sunday and a few other 'spiritual' things. Spirituality encompasses all realms of life including the economic realm.

2. Human acts usually have a financial component
In *Godly Materialism,* John Schneider writes: "All the great acts of God were economic events."[20]

Starting in the Garden of Eden, God said, "Be fruitful and increase in number; fill the earth and subdue it."[21] Managing the earth is an economic act. It was the first act God commanded humankind to do.

Pick a Biblical story and more likely than not, you will find an economic connection involving some form of management of economic reality. And the teachings of Christ are full of illustrations on wise and foolish management of money. The Apostle Paul put things in perspective by saying "If a man will not work, he shall not eat."[22]

From Genesis to Revelation, The Bible is clear that God's reality involves an economic reality.

3. Economics are congruent with God's principles
As you work to achieve your vision, you engage God in the process *he* started in your heart. It follows that the financial aspects of your vision need to be congruent with God's principles.

As I've said before, your vision involves work. If your vision is legitimate, it is also part of God's work. The book *Your Work Matters to God* tells its readers: "All legitimate work is an extension of God's work."[23] That means your vision is hardly beneath God's dignity and concern. As you work to achieve your vision, keep your view of finances and financial management congruent with God's principles of economic management.

4. Economics are part of redeeming a broken world
The teachings and acts of Christ are centered on redemption. First and foremost is the redemption of bringing fallen individuals back to God—the restoring of relationship. In addition you see redemption of the psychological, social, political, environmental and all other aspects of our earthly reality: including an economic redemption.

Christ's teachings are full of examples of gaining a correct economic perspective. He said, "One's life does not consist in the abundance of possessions."[24] Your value is not attached to your bank account and stock options. It comes from something different. He talks about the rich official and how riches clouded his ability to see. Money was the root of all sorts of evil in the man's thinking.[25]

On another economic subject, Christ taught about foolish and wise stewards of money. In Matthew 25, he tells of a man who went on a journey and entrusted money to three of his servants, each according to his ability. Two invested the money and gained more. The other servant, because of fear and laziness, did nothing with the money—the talents. His master reprimanded him:

"You wicked, lazy servant! So you knew that I harvest where I have not sown and gather where I have not scattered seed? Well then, you should have put my money on deposit with the bankers, so that when I returned I would have received it back with interest.

"Take the talent from him and give it to the one who has the ten talents. For everyone who has will be given more, and he will have an abundance. Whoever does not have, even what he has will be taken from him. And throw that worthless servant outside, into the darkness, where there will be weeping and gnashing of teeth."[26]

By telling this parable, Christ challenged people to be proactive in managing financial assets and warned against a spirit of timidity in response to the economic world. He called his people to enter the world and enlarge the master's power and dominion within it.

God wants for you to be proactive and wise when managing any assets related toward the achievement of your vision.

#

Be careful not to look at reality through distorted glasses. Don't follow the ancient Greek view of separating the ideal ('spiritual') from the physical, when in fact the Biblical view melds the seen and the unseen—neither is to be ignored, minimized, or treated in a sloppy manner. The Bible calls you to bring the lordship of Christ into all areas of reality, including the economic realities.

Questions:

15:1 Go back and look at View #1: What is your worldview concerning money and God?

15:2 Go back and look at View #2: Do you operate from the 'Reward Model'? Examine your financial relationship to God and your expectations of Him.

DAY 16

FROM WALLETS, BANK ACCOUNTS, BENEATH THE MATTRESS

Money never starts an idea; it is the idea that starts the money.
W. J. Cameron

Unless you win the lottery or come into a surprise inheritance today, you have to find funding to support your vision. If you can already bankroll the first actions or even the complete process of your vision, you still have to manage your money wisely.

Many new vision builders immediately get carried away with spreadsheets, profit-and-loss statements, balance sheets, pricing specifics, product cost comparisons, and so on. I certainly have done this on several projects, to the point that the spreadsheets became an elaborate imaginary world of their own. You may eventually address these things, but I suggest that you hold off for now. Complex financial models can come later, but just start by considering the basics.

Start by answering the following three questions. Note that though they look simple, they require some effort now and even more later:

1. What monies do you need to kick-start your vision?

Notice that the question involves two parts: the beginning and the ongoing. I'd advise you to not neglect either part, because each will have different complexities. Many initial expenses may not recur, whereas downstream, you may have regular periodic costs such as salaries, rent, fees, etc.

You have to know what finances you will need. How much will it cost you to get your vision going—what are your start-up costs? And once you have begun, how much will it cost to keep your vision going?

If you plan to start a business, you need to know how much money is necessary for marketing, salaries, production and administration. If you plan to start a sculpture studio, how much money do you need to support yourself while you work? How much do you need for supplies, studio rent, exhibition entry fees?

You get the picture. And the picture will be different for every vision. But whether your expenses are ten dollars or ten million, you need to realistically address the financial reality of your vision.

2. Where will the money come from now and later?

A job-training center, a church Bible study, a international import-export business. For each of these and any other visions, you need to know your sources of revenue.

Where will you get the money to get started? Your own pocket? Friends and family? A venture capitalist? An organization? Organizations can be associations, churches, philanthropic foundations, non-profits, or governmental agencies.

You need to know exactly how you will gain access to that money, how you will approach the decision makers who would give it to you, and what kind of paper work you need. Without the assurance of that funding, your project is unlikely to come to life.

And just getting the funding for the initial phase isn't enough. Additional phases will require funding. Say your vision is to go back to university and complete your degree and then to embark on a new profession. You may be funding your first semester through your own savings, but after that, your bank account will be at zero. Before or during your first semester, you will have to focus on applying for scholarships or loans.

Or you may take on a part-time job. And once you obtain your degree and enter your new profession, your funding model changes again.

3. Are you covered?

Will your vision create enough revenue to cover your expenses? If not, what will you do?

Once you know your overall financial requirements and where the funding is coming from, you need to know if there will be enough money to cover your expenses. If not, then you have a problem and need to solve it. In business terms, you need to figure out your break-even point: the point at which the funding will cover your costs.

If you are business savvy, you may be skimming along and thinking this is all obvious. But you might be surprised how many businessmen I've met who are in deep personal debt, splurge on whims and have not adequately invested for the future. While they may be adept at managing a company, their own finances are in shambles. They haven't considered these simple questions for their personal lives, and their credit card debt shows it.

Does the way you are spending your money reflect your vision priorities? Is buying that boat, designer dress, set of golf clubs or new bedroom set a part of your vision? If not you will have to finance them by working to pay a bill instead of working toward your goal.

If you tend to spend irresponsibly or neglect your financial circumstances, watch out. Continuing with poor money management habits will endanger the birth, let alone the life of your vision.

Answer these questions and get control of your finances. If you don't, you can kiss your vision goodbye.

Questions:

16:1 What monies do you need to kick-start your vision? To keep it going?

16:2 Where will the money come from now and later?

16:3 Are you covered? If not, what are you going to do about it?

Action Three
Manage the Stages with Wisdom

DAY 17
SETTING THE STAGES

A sluggard does not plow in season; so at harvest time he looks but finds nothing. Proverbs 20:4

The plans of the diligent lead to profit as surely as haste leads to poverty. Proverbs 21:5

These two Proverbs compare the sluggard and the diligent person. But they also convey a sense of timing.

Simply put, the sluggard doesn't prepare the ground at the right time — at the beginning of the growing season. Compare this with the diligent person who makes plans which then lead to profit. The diligent person is not hasty, but carefully plans and manages.

I would like you to apply the 'diligent' approach to your visionary endeavor by presenting you with four different stages for achieving your vision. They are sequential and most likely you will have to expend some effort to journey through them. Be sure to accomplish each stage before moving on to the next.

The stages:

1. **Concept**
2. **Development**
3. **Establishment**
4. **Growth**

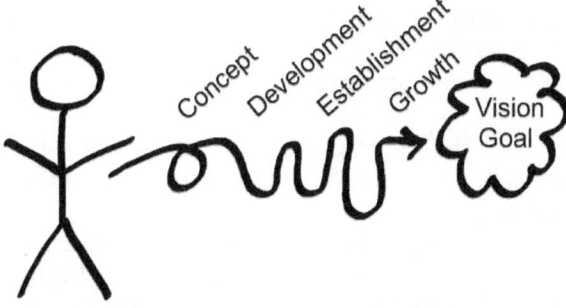

A word of encouragement: the risk level for achieving your vision changes as you pass through each stage. This means that the possibility and likelihood of reaching your vision increases as you move along the list. Most vision quests will fit within this model, but not all. Depending on the vision, you may notice overlap between the stages, but generally they remain distinct.

It is important to keep in mind that the plan and the journey are not played out on a straight line:

I have used the illustration of your visionary journey as a story that begins when you enter the forest. Any good story has its ups and downs—remember that as you action from stage to stage. Consider these stages the four section headings to your story:

Stage One: Concept

Guess what? You've already started. The concept stage develops your vision. It begins with the act of answering all the questions found in actions one and two. It is defining your vision and how you will bring it to life by building the necessary conceptual framework.

If your goal were to build a physical product, this stage also involves building a prototype to see if it actually works. It involves considering, analyzing and getting specific about who would be using that product. It's about managing the construction of your concept.

But you can't just stay in your own head here. You've got to test your concept—Alpha testing. Get it to other people, whether it be a group, experts in your field, or potential recipients of your product or service. Identify and engage with these people.

This will allow you to reach the milestone of stage one: proof of principle. This basically means that you can only move on to stage two if the experts or recipients agree that your idea has merit. If they do not agree, listen carefully as to why, and then go back and make necessary adjustments.

At this point, you have to evaluate whether you should continue to pursue your vision. It is difficult to say to yourself *my idea was interesting, but maybe it lacks validity*. Still, it's better to stop before you waste any more time and money on an endeavor that will ultimately fail.

Before despairing, use the advice from your experts and recipients to adapt your conceptual model as creatively as possible. Then test it again with them.

John has a vision to help high school students in low-income neighborhoods prepare for university. He knows that higher education is one means of breaking the poverty cycle, and he wants to help students prepare for the entrance exams, select and apply for entrance to colleges, and seek out financial aid. He plans to engage a network of volunteers to help with this. As he brings his idea into the real world he plans to start by using facilities in an existing church and eventually expanding to other churches and office spaces in close proximity to his target users.

John's proof of principle is to get the approval of his church leaders to use the church building. It is engaging one or two volunteers and finding a few potential recipients of his service to test it in action, in reality. The proof of principle is also a matter of John asking for feedback from those leaders, volunteers and students about his concept. Armed with their suggestions, he can adjust his concept and better prepare it for stage two's development.

Another thing about the concept stage: in most cases you will probably fund it yourself unless it is a large and complex idea requiring extensive resources. Friends and family might also be backing you at this stage.

The risk level is highest here. In the world of startup companies, the concept stage is where you face the greatest difficulty in raising money from outside investors. If individual 'angel' investors or venture capitalists come in at this stage, they know the enormous risk. Therefore they will ask for a large stake in the equity of the endeavor.

Finish the conceptual framework of your vision by running an Alpha test—your proof of principle. If your vision is a product, get a prototype made, see if it actually works, and get expert advice on it. If your vision is a service, get your concept on paper and ask for suggestions about it, especially from the people who would be involved (like John's church leaders and volunteers) as well as your potential recipients.

Once you do, congratulations. You are on your way to actually achieving your vision.

Stage Two: Development

Now you get to assemble the infrastructure to support your vision. In this stage, you bring your concept into reality. That's why you need infrastructure and the flexibility to change it as it makes contact with reality.

Let's revisit John's college-prep service from stage one. John's church allowed him to use one of their ministry rooms, his two friends volunteered to help tutor, and he found seven student volunteers. With those factors established, he began his Beta test not long after the school year commenced. By late winter, six of the students had remained with the program, and all had applied to college. All of them were accepted, and two received sizable scholarships.

John's Beta testing was positive. Only at that point was he able to broaden the advising program for the following year. It would have been unwise to do so if his test students had not benefited from it, if his volunteers had not shown up, or if the church had been unable to let him use its facilities.

Don't move forward and expand if you have major adjustments to make. The milestone of the development stage is acceptance by your recipients.

A word on funding: this stage may begin to be funded by external sources—most likely from interested individuals rather than organizations. People who invest in your vision at this stage will still be expecting a high equity stake, or ownership.

For those of you starting humanitarian or social projects, you will often find individuals with a strong interest in your vision. These people are willing to give money philanthropically—they are not looking for a direct return on investment.

The risk level starts to decline in this stage. Though the development stage often requires the most groundwork for establishing initial infrastructure, it has moved beyond the point of pure concept. You are now implementing your idea in the real world and demonstrating its validity.

But you're not there yet.

Stage Three: Establishment

In this stage you are establishing your concept. Stage two required select acceptance by test recipients, stage three requires general acceptance by your target recipients.

Following the success of his Beta testing, John went on to raise local funding to buy study guides and software to prepare students for standardized aptitude tests. He found a church willing to let him use their youth room a couple of blocks around the corner from the high school where he tested. He asked his test recipients to tell their friends about their experience while he looked for ways of reaching other students. He posted fliers and arranged with the principle to speak at the opening assembly of the school year to reach his target recipients.

This is marketing. I realize that this term has become something of a 'bad' word, seen as a means of wrongly manipulating people. I am using it in the context of understanding people's needs and communicating the benefits of your idea to reach those needs.

Because of his marketing, John was able to enlist two dozen students for his advising program. If he had merely sat in the church foyer waiting for them to walk in, he would not have had any success.

The key milestone here is general acceptance by your target market. That means there are people who want your product or service. If your vision is commercial, your milestone is 'Invoice

#001'. If it is a humanitarian or social project, your milestone is when the target recipients are benefiting from your service and donors have agreed to provide the ongoing funding to keep your organization running.

The risk level in this stage begins to drop. Your vision idea has started to prove itself. It is succeeding. But you guessed it: the work doesn't stop here.

Stage Four: Growth

The growth stage takes on an entirely different complexity. Here, you have brought your vision to life. Now it is a matter of keeping it alive. To do this, you need to consider these business-sounding aspects:

- **Processes**
- **Organization**
- **Management**
- **Production**
- **Market development**
- **Product/Service enhancement**

Sound far too complicated? It's not. By the time you're here, this stuff is happening and you are addressing it. This is the stage where our visionary John is engaging more churches and organizations to assist with afternoon and early evening counseling services to students. This is where he is enlisting more volunteers, coordinating their schedules, continuing to communicate with the students in the target group. The growth stage is an expansion of the operations to meet his initial vision of making a difference in the economics of a poor community.

In this stage your key milestone is viability of the endeavor. This goes beyond breaking even or even making a profit: you have brought your vision to life and now you get to build that vision and/or move on to something new.

Your risk level has dramatically decreased. If your vision was a commercial endeavor, it will begin to command the highest return on investment. If your vision is non-commercial, its structure is up and running, or you have come to the end of your quest and ready to use this as a stepping-stone to the next journey.

#

You cannot sidestep these stages. Manage them wisely and carefully, one after the other. As the Proverb said, you can't move too hastily through them, or your vision will not be realized. Remember to focus on each key objective and milestone while keeping the next stage in mind.

Questions

17:1 What stage is your vision in? Detail your current focus, milestone and funding source.

17:2 What is the next major milestone you need to achieve that will allow you to move onto the next stage? Be as exact as possible.

DAY 18
ESSENTIALS FOR TASKING

Start by doing what's necessary; then do what's possible; and suddenly you are doing the impossible   Saint Francis of Assisi

You could view the stages in the last chapter something like this:

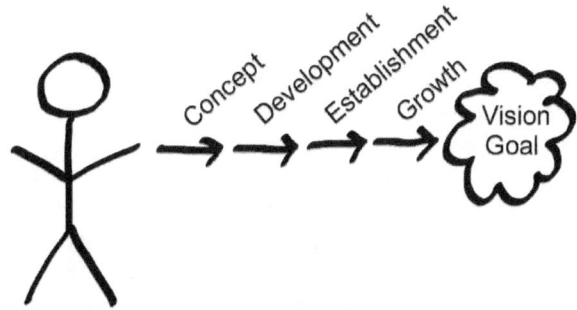

Each stage needs to be broken down into a series of actions or tasks in order to achieve your milestone.

Simpler visions may involve only one or two tasks in each stage, while more complex visions might involve dozens. You are the one who will have to decide what tasks need to be done and to do them — or assign them to others.

To assist with that process, I'd like to give you some ideas for managing whatever tasks arise in your vision.

Guess or test?
Unless you are a Biblical prophet, any projections you make into the future are on a best-guess basis. The specific plans you make (tasks) in each stage are your approximation of what it will take to move your vision project forward.

In the context of starting new ventures, Donald Sull suggests that each action of a project be thought of as hypothesis testing.[27] Consider every planned task within each stage as a set of experimentations. Ask yourself at each step: *what am I trying to test or accomplish?* Depending on the results of testing, the vision builder may revise the hypothesis and run another 'experiment.' In other words, to bring your vision into reality, you may have to backtrack and tweak things.

Say you are in the concept stage for a service. You want to start a book discussion group to get your neighbors to know each other. However, the potential recipients you spoke with—your neighbors—don't have time to read books but like the idea of getting together. You need to revise your concept and find an activity that they have time to enjoy. Your concept/plan is not set in stone. Remember to be flexible.

View each task as experimentation—but keep attentive. Carefully evaluate each task as you progress through it. If necessary, modify and retrace your actions.

Ready, set, step . . . in faith
On the surface, it might seem discouraging to operate from a best-guess standpoint. But when you do, you are in fact stepping forward in faith into the unknown. In life, if you knew exactly what to do and exactly what to expect, you wouldn't need much faith. It's the same in implementing a vision—or any other endeavor.

Now the question is: what do you put your faith in? Is that task purely a material manipulation of facts and objects, or does it engage God? Where and in what is your faith as you move through each task and stage?

Oliver Cromwell, the Puritan who led a civil revolt against the king of England, is said to have told his troops to "trust in God and keep your powder dry." God expects trust. But if your gun is gummed up with moisture due to inattentiveness, forget hitting your target. Be responsible and proactive within trust.

Align your resources before each task
Know what resources you need before beginning each task. Your ideal situation is to have those necessary resources in place and aligned before you even begin a task. But don't be surprised to look back and see that some "essentials" you invested in turned out to be useless. As I've said, you can't predict the future.

Get funding plus buffers
How much funding will you need for each stage and each task within it? Should you raise enough money to cover the entire project, or just enough to cover the next action?

From my experience, I recommend the latter. And also from experience, I can tell you that there will be some anxiety involved. With an initial chunk of raised money, you can easily feel rich and misuse the funds, and your investors will be asking for a huge equity stake. Plus, things will change along the way and you'll face difficulties if you have to renegotiate the investor's expectations. They may even take the project away from you.

As each project stage succeeds, it becomes easier to engage more investors if needed. And with each successful stage, you have the chance to think through the best funding model—which may not be evident when you begin the project. Still, don't wait too long to raise money. It takes time. Think ahead.

Consider outsourcing

If you are busy trying to start a cafe, you don't want to waste time washing windows if you have to train employees and meet with coffee distributors on a deadline. Outsource. Pay someone else to do non-critical tasks. The money you spend is actually an investment in your vision, because it frees time for the essential tasks within the stages of your vision. At each stage examine the necessary tasks and see what someone else can do. Professional window washers, accountants, and electricians also had a vision: they saw a need and sought to fill it. Use them.

Are you getting carried away?

In almost any vision-building project, I have seen a distinct danger. I call this decision-making blunder 'the expediency of the moment.' It happens when you make short-term decisions without adequately thinking about the long-term needs of your vision project.

Say you need a partner. Partnerships can be risky. I have been involved in projects where we brought someone on board to meet an immediate need, gave the person an equity stake in the enterprise, and then painfully realized that the new partner did not match the long-term goals of the enterprise.

Expediency-of-the-moment issues arise in all arenas. You may be in the check-out line at an electronics superstore and see an all-in-one printer, fax, copier, scanner on a special holiday sale that you 'just can't pass up.' You may think that you can't live without that software in the catalog. And you're sure that if you don't fly three states away to attend that trade convention you'll miss out on pertinent information for your startup.

Days, weeks, or months later, you find yourself admitting that the all-in-one printer is a lousy scanner and makes hideously slow copies, your accountant is ten times better than the software, and the only thing you got out of the convention were a few more frequent flier miles.

The problem is that the 'need' of the moment can take on an entire life of its own. Some people treat each need as supreme, neglecting to think about its long-term impact. They go from need to need, moment by moment.

As you move through the stages from task to task, remember that each action is a small part of your larger vision. Take your time, stand back from each perceived need and balance it against the long-term requirements of your endeavor. Don't be led astray by the expediency of the moment.

Questions:

18:1 Go back to your answers to last chapter's questions. What are the specific tasks required to achieve the major milestone you have set for that stage?

18:2 What is the very next task you need to accomplish?

Action Four ▶
Set and Achieve Targets

DAY 19
TARGETS AND DATES

Make no little plans. They have no magic to stir men's blood and probably themselves will not be realized. Make big plans. Aim high in hope and work. Remembering that a noble, logical diagram once recorded will not die. Daniel H. Burnham *Architect, Leader of the Chicago School*

Now you get to set targets and dates for each task and then for each major milestone. This is the deadline stuff that will keep you on track. Without concrete details, your vision will just float out there awaiting your command. It is one thing to have a concept. It is another to actually make it happen.

Targets

Tasks are things you need to do. A target is a way of measuring the task and setting a deadline for making it happen. Without getting into a semantic discussion I would like to use 'target' as a specific and measurable aim related to your vision. In other words, it is your task—with some specifics added.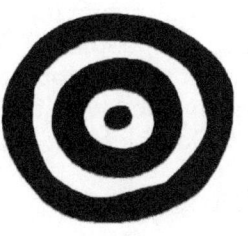

Different planning methodologies give different values to words like: objective, goal and target. Often an objective is seen as a broad statement describing a desired future condition or achievement. It's usually not too specific about 'how much' and 'when.' You want to be more detailed. Plus, as I've said, an objective can sound dry. Your vision is personal, passionate and motivational—hardly dry. It is more than an objective.

Targets are quantitative and measurable—a performance goal to be achieved by a given time. You could say Michael's target was to get to the airport on time to catch the 8:00 p.m. flight. Targets support your vision.

Dates

To further quantify the target you need to set some dates and timelines. If you have put a schedule in place, when will each action within the schedule take place? What is the final deadline for attaining that task or reaching the milestone for the phase?

Joanne established a schedule with dates related to the target. On Wednesday, she planned to stop by the bank to get the loan papers. On Thursday evening she would fill out the papers, and on Friday she would obtain the loan: her target.

Measurements
A good target can be measured, quantified. You can measure if indeed Michael caught his 8 p.m. flight and if Joanne picked up the loan papers on Wednesday, filled them in on Thursday and met with the banker on Friday. Another measuring stick: did she end up obtaining the loan? And you can measure her overall goal: did she buy a house?

The point is, at some point of review in the future you need to be able to look back and evaluate whether you did meet your targets. To do this, you have to hold them up against some standard of quantification.

Responsibility
A final aspect of a good target is the person responsible for achieving it. Since your vision is your own, you will likely be the responsible one. But achieving your vision might require a partnership, or a team of people, or those hired for outsourced tasks. If you don't assign responsibilities, then tasks can fall between the cracks. That means they won't happen on time, if at all.

Don't let that happen.

Questions:

19:1 Are your tasks measurable? If not can you redefine them to be so?

19:2 By what exact dates will you accomplish your tasks?

19:3 Who is responsible for achieving each task?

Action Five ▶
Be Accountable

DAY 20
CONFIDE AND CONSULT

The secret of man is the secret of his responsibility.
Václav Havel

Why be accountable to someone? For all the reasons you've read thus far; because your journey will have its ups and downs, because you will have to address the pressures and enemies working against you, because of your existing patterns of behavior, because your motivation level will fluctuate.

Even though you are more or less your own "boss" on your visionary journey, it is extremely helpful to be accountable to someone. That can simply mean meeting with a friend or confidant regularly. It helps, of course, if that person is willing to stick with you through your quest.

This confidant should, as the name implies, be someone you can confide in. Your vision project is about you, and as you progress through it, you will discover things about yourself. When you find yourself stumbling through weaknesses and struggles, it helps to know that someone is there to listen and even advise.

So the role not only involves confiding, but consulting. Choose someone you know is able to carefully listen and help you see things from a different angle. Someone who will keep you on your toes.

The person you are accountable to may be a partner, a friend, family member, or leader in your church. They should be sympathetic to your vision and may even already be assisting with it. I know that I am far more motivated to get to the gym or weed the garden if my wife and I have arranged to do so together. Whenever a few compatible people are struggling together to achieve a cause, they are more likely to be motivated to accomplish it. Why? Because they are accountable to each other.

But a caveat here: it helps if this person is not directly engaged in the project. Don't have your business partner play this role. Find an outside source for advice whom you both respect. You need a sounding board. You need a different perspective on things to maintain a degree of objectivity.

Depending on your personality, be careful who you choose. If you are timid, don't fall back on the perceived safety of someone whose 'advise' is really dictation in disguise. You don't want to walk away from a discussion feeling unduly guilty for not having reached a target or milestone as originally planned. If you are more overriding, don't choose the easy someone who will nod and congratulate every task even when there are obvious problems to confront. You need someone to ask the hard questions. You know you'll need to answer them.

Once you find your 'consultant,' agree to meet regularly. Schedule the days and times in a calendar. Invite the person over for tea or coffee and clarify exactly what you would like them to do. I advise that you don't contact your consultant too often — you don't want to wear out your welcome. Meeting just after you expect to achieve major milestones is a good system. Then you can review the process and evaluate what went right and wrong, what you learned, and delineate the tasks needed to meet the next milestone.

And when you have successfully brought your vision to life, treat your consultant to something special.

Question:

20:1 Who will you be accountable to?

DAY 21
KEEP YOUR SECRETS

Beware before you share!

Being accountable to your consultant about your vision means sharing your ideas and plans. This is where I want to emphasize trust. You *must* be able to trust this person. This is where the secrecy of your vision comes to play.

Your vision belongs to you. Be careful about sharing it with anyone, and be careful about when you release your information. In North American culture, people are often open with each other and tend to immediately divulge plans and projects.

Having lived in Northern Europe for years, I've observed quite a difference in information sharing between there and North America. On any given domestic US flight, two strangers seated next to each other will soon start to share how many children they have, why they are taking the trip, even their hopes and desires — all personal topics that the average Northern European would be reluctant to divulge.

If you live in North America, you know that information flows quickly and easily. It is a country at the forefront of the information superhighway. Wherever you live, I'd advise you to take a very different approach when it comes to sharing your vision. Why? Read on.

Someone can steal your idea

People copy good ideas. Before your plane taxis to the arrival gate, the former stranger next to you, Bob, may already be devising a way to create the kitchen gizmo you described with such enthusiasm. Because, yes, it's a great idea. And Bob may nab the resources you were expecting to draw into your project. He may even have more startup capital than you. Bam: now there's competition and an enormous hassle you could have avoided if you had kept the idea to yourself.

In the business world you have a Non-Disclosure Agreement or 'NDA.' With this agreement, one party consents to not disclose information that the other party has shared with them — information usually related to products or a business plan. If your vision idea is to create a sell-able product or start a company, I advise you to have people sign a NDA before you share too many confidential details with them. If your vision is not commercial, still be very careful. Other people can steal your idea.

Your credibility is at risk

When you share your vision, you expose yourself. People immediately have expectations of you. But what if your vision needs further refinement? What if you tell potential investors about your plan to start a wilderness camp for troubled teens and then end up opening an organic juice bar? You come across as unstable or even untrustworthy. You have exposed yourself and your credibility is at risk.

Information overload damages your vision

Be careful how you release the information on your vision. Don't tell everything all at once if you don't have to. If you need to persuade people to gain their commitment, drip them information drop by drop. This gives them time to think about it. There may be 'politics' attached to who, how, and when you tell others about what you want to do.

Early on, decide how much information you want to share and at what times. Sometimes people respond best to an idea when they have time to warm up to it, especially if they don't understand it or its implications initially. By not telling everything about your vision to everybody, you also have a chance to get feedback from them and make modifications.

If you release the wrong information to the wrong person at the wrong time, that person may undermine you by starting unnecessary rumors. All kinds of unexpected backlash may come out of this. Don't go seeking ridicule and rejection.

#

I discussed the vision-builder Nehemiah earlier. When he arrived in Jerusalem, he walked around the city, looked at the city walls, and didn't tell anyone what he was up to. He knew there might be enemies who would try to stop him, and there were. He also needed to gain the confidence of the Jewish leaders of the city.

Their commitment was necessary to rebuild the walls.

The point is, don't give everything away to everyone all at once, or even to individual people with whom you are not entirely confident. Wisely manage the information flow of your vision. Beware before you share!

Question:

21:1 What are your tendencies when it comes to divulging information? Are you likely to give away too much and if so, how can you remind yourself to keep your secrets?

Action Six ▶
Take Action

DAY 22
ACT NOW!

There is one thing stronger than all the armies of the world: that is an idea whose time has come.   Victor Hugo

Until now, you have been forming your vision on a conceptual level and hopefully getting ready to develop it. It's time 'to action out of the box' and begin your journey.

Let's pick up with Nehemiah again. When he first heard about the conditions in the city of Jerusalem, he was deeply troubled and prayed about the circumstance for several months. Through this time he developed a vision to go back, rebuild the walls, and redeem the city. Then he had an opportunity to share this with the king, and the king gave him a green light.

Up until the moment he shared with the king, Nehemiah's vision remained primarily conceptual. But he was not passive prior to that. During those previous months, he had been bringing his concern to God in prayer. When he stood before the king, he took a risk. He said, "I had to gather up my courage." That risk was stepping out of the routine, the expected, by sharing his desires with the king. At that moment, he began to move out of the box.

I think Nehemiah's real moment of truth came the day that he walked away from Susa, the capital city of the empire where he had been living. He left a secure job working directly for the most powerful man in the kingdom. Now he faced a long journey to get to Jerusalem. Imagine him as he traveled, either on foot or on a donkey or camel. I can just see him turning around and looking back at the splendor of Susa. Then he looks forward at the vast desert in front of him, and he asks himself, "what in the world am I doing?"

That's what happens when you action out into the unknown.

Piece together Nehemiah's visionary process: He heard of a need in Jerusalem, he had a vision to meet that need and took it to God in prayer. He shared his vision with the king—who happened to approve of Nehemiah's venture. Then you can assume he prepared for the journey by gathering the necessary resources, and finally the day came that he stepped out of Susa on a committed quest. It was there that his adventure began.

Ask yourself of your vision: *what is the first action I will take to achieve my vision and when will I take it?* Don't panic. That first action doesn't have to be a big one. You just have to get the momentum going. Maybe you set up a meeting. Maybe you go to the library or get on the internet and commence research. Maybe you fill out some forms and send them off.

The first action you take is like tipping the first domino at the head of a great big line of them. All you have to do is push over the first one to precipitate a chain of events—the falling of the dominos.

However, unlike a line of dominos where the action and reaction is rather predictable, the events of your quest involve uncertainty. But you can't plan for everything. You simply have to go for it.

I advise you to do it now. Sooner rather than later. If you let your idea sit there without taking action, then it will either stay inert and useless, or someone else will come along and do it. I ask you: what can you do today, in the next hour? Now? Do it.

If your vision is the most imperative thing you want to accomplish, shouldn't most of your thoughts and actions be focused on achieving it? If your vision is as important and necessary as you have realized it is, why isn't your next action connected to implementing your vision?

Get moving!

Questions:

21:1 What is the very next action you will take to start the momentum to achieve your vision?

21:2 When will you do it?

Action Seven ▶
Get the Spiritual Implications

DAY 23
DISTINCTIVE SERVICE

All of us have a 'unique eternal calling to count for good in God's great universe.' Dallas Willard

Many people have asked me why I add the action of comprehending spiritual implications. "Aren't you a businessman?", they ask. "Why do you start talking about theology?" I do this because I believe it is important to have a spiritual context for your vision and to know how it fits within the broader theme of service.

Why? When you are aware of this, your vision is anchored in a more holistic view of reality, a higher level of meaning. When you face doubts and barriers as you bring your vision to life, holding fast to these spiritual implications helps you continue.

Here's how I see it.

When you begin a job at a company, you are often given a job description that outlines the title of your position, a summary of the role you will play in the company, a list of the tasks you will perform, and the requirements you need to accomplish them.

All human beings have a fundamental job description consisting of two parts. The first is your general role, something you universally share with everyone. This calls for all people to live lives of faith in relationship with God while cultivating and redeeming the world. It includes a general calling to be a responsible member of God's creation. I referred to this back when I described Couple Number Two who started the church outside of Geneva.

The other part, your distinctive role, is unique to you. With this you apply your individual interests and capabilities to the particular activities to which you are called, including your vision.

Both of these roles entail the inauguration of the kingdom of God in our world, that is, bringing the lordship of Christ into every aspect of life and living accordingly. As Michael Novak wrote:

We start here on earth what will be fulfilled in heaven. The creator did not make the world finished, but to be finished. His purpose in making women and men in his image was to draw them into his own creative work as co-creators.[28]

If your vision fits your general and distinctive callings—your job description—then it will be most rewarding because it is congruent with your basic purpose. If your vision falls outside these roles, then you will find an inherent misalignment between your fundamental job description and your vision. If this is the case, your identity will not be validated. Here are several reasons why:

You are created in God's image

In the first chapter of Genesis God is, quite literally, creative. He moves in the midst of a formless space, he speaks, and he creates light. But he doesn't stop there. He starts making things on an immense scale. He creates sky, mountain, humans. He creates a universe of both the seen and the unseen.

After you read about that initial creation, you learn that humans are unique from the rest of creation in that they are made in God's image. He gave humans the ability to communicate and love, to innovate and create. As Paul Stevens pointed out, Adam's first act is one of innovation; he names the animals.[29]

Because you are created in God's image, that image is the foundation for your identity.

You are created to keep and advance the garden

The mandate God has given to all people is to care and enhance the world. This calling originates from the first role given to humans. Early in the book of Genesis it says, "Then the Lord God took the man and put him into the Garden of Eden to cultivate it and keep it." Genesis 2:15. That's the original job description.

Some might say this was a specific task given to Adam, yet principles throughout the Bible support that this commandment continually applies to all humans. And it entails more than simply cultivating a physical garden. God desires that humans tend to the totality of reality with all of its physical, social, economic and spiritual realms.

Your general role "to cultivate and keep the garden" defines your identity. And your vision must align with this role.

You are called to redeem a broken world

The original mandate of cultivating the garden is still valid for humans today. But there came along an interfering problem: evil. Because of it, this world is broken and fallen. Also because of it, the original mandate expanded.

So along with being called to care for the fallen world, each human is also now called to redeem the fallen world — to restore it into a right relationship with God and make it better. The Bible is rich with examples of this: everything from caring for the poor, repairing social and political systems, spiritual restoration, etc.

Foundational to this, we must remember that God continues

to redeem his creation. Though the universe is broken because of rebellion against God, he reaches out in love to call people back to him. Of course the greatest redemptive act was when Christ paid the penalty for our rebellion by dying on the cross. We can't add anything to this by believing we need to do something extra to win God's favor. It is God through his grace and love who has enabled us to reenter a direct relationship with him.

This access to God is not passive. It is an active calling to participate with him in that innovation and redemption. We are called to participate with him in redeeming a broken world.

You are called to inaugurate the kingdom of God

Redeeming the world — restoring and making it better — is required, but it is not the end of the story. It must be seen in the context of inaugurating the kingdom of God. The teachings and acts of Christ are first and foremost about this. Jesus didn't come to earth merely to redeem people but also to announce and enact the arrival of God's long awaited reign. Just have a look at the parables. The kingdom of God is in most of them. It is central to Christ's teaching. We are to work to establish God's reign in our broken world, and to look forward to the time when he returns and his kingdom will be fully established.

Your vision is not God. Your vision is something to be brought before God and then positioned within his reign and kingdom. While it is okay to be highly passionate, even obsessed by your vision, do not let it replace God. Vision is subservient to God and needs to be positioned accordingly. His lordship applies to every corner of your life, including your vision.

You gain personal joy through innovation

Being innovative can provide you with personal joy and fulfillment. This is evident when you observe God's reaction after creating the heavens and the earth. At the end of the first day in which he had made light, God stood back, took a look and saw that it was good. At the end of the sixth day, he saw that all he had made was "very good". Amazingly, because you are created in God's image, you can have a similar sense of satisfaction in your work.

Painting the doors of my house a new color is hardly comparable to creating a universe, but when I stand back and look at them, I derive a great sense of satisfaction at the completed job. They look good. That same sense of satisfaction can come through the completion of many of our works, especially those involving creativity and innovation.

This joy also arises during the process of doing the work, not just when we action back and smile at the finished product.

I identify with God's characteristics as a worker and feel linked to him when engaging in work.

Remember that as you pursue your vision, you can experience great joy *while* you work to attain it, not just when you finally see it accomplished.

You are holding a unique purpose and vision

The Reformers believed that all professions were noble and contained dignity. Think about the following quotes within the context of your vision.

William Tyndale, the first person to translate the Bible from its original languages into English, and was martyred for it, said, "If we look externally, there is a difference between washing of dishes and preaching the word of God, but as touching to please God, none at all."[30]

Ulrich Zwingli, another Reformer, said, "There is nothing in the universe so like God as the worker."[31]

John Calvin brought this into the context of one's unique calling when he said, "The Lord bids each one of us in all life's actions to look to his calling . . . no task will be so sordid and base, that it will not shine and be reckoned very precious in God's sight."[32]

William Perkins, a Puritan writer and teacher followed Calvin's thinking by stating that, "The action of the shepherd in keeping sheep is as good a work before God as the action of a judge in giving sentence, or of a magistrate in ruling, or a minister in preaching. Thus then we see there is a good reason why we would search how every man is rightly to use his particular calling.[33]"

Each of these statements come from Christian leaders who continue to be highly respected today. Each leader is saying that God values every person's distinctive occupation, and therefore each job—and the work done within it—has dignity and meaning. (Of course, these leaders spoke against certain occupations that did not provide a positive service, such as prostitution.)

This also means that your vision, as your particular calling, has meaning and dignity before God. Unfortunately, some Christians teach, either implicitly or explicitly, that certain activities or professions are valued more than others. Often, the top of the hierarchy is occupied by the missionary, followed by the evangelist or pastor, and then all other occupations. These 'lower-level' occupations are given value only because they fund the 'higher-level' occupations. Sadly, they are rarely given dignity as they are. But our purpose is *to cultivate and redeem the world around us.* That means that all occupations (and visions) hold equal dignity when they fulfill this role.

#

As you bring your vision to life, remember that your job description is composed of your general and distinctive roles of service. Those roles are the spiritual context for your vision.

Questions:

23:1 Does your vision fit both your general and distinctive calling?

23:2 How do you live your life with redemption in mind?

DAY 24
IN THE SPIRIT

Vision looks inwards and becomes duty. Vision looks outwards and becomes aspiration. Vision looks upwards and becomes faith.
Stephen S. Wise

Viewing your project in a spiritual light will help you recall its importance and will continue to motivate you when the stress levels soar, the bills come all at once, and you find yourself wondering if you took the right path.

Review a few considerations with me to firmly position your vision in God's plan for your life.

It's redeeming and transforming

Now that you have formulated a plan and have hopefully even started to implement that plan, I suggest that you revisit your answers to the questions about the redeeming nature of your vision. Can you articulate how your project will not only care for and redeem the world, but also make it better?

It's about your faith

For this consideration, I'd like to ask you some questions:

How will you apply your personal spirituality to the journey?

What is your worldview as you journey through your vision?

Are you keeping in mind the unseen reality? The God who is there? Are you going to engage with God at each step of the journey?

Will you include God in your understanding and decision-making, acknowledge him, and trust him to make the path clear? Or are you going to do this on your own?

How do you expect your faith to grow on this journey?

Your character will be tested; are you going to look at that as an opportunity for your faith to be tested too?

Only you can answer these questions. Remembering to ask them of yourself along the way will make that way much more rewarding.

It's personal

Lastly, while this goal you have chosen for yourself may make a difference out in the world, what difference will it make for you personally? How is it going to affect your spirituality? Why is your vision so important to you?

Questions:

24:1 Now that you have formulated your vision and your plan, can you articulate the redemptive qualities of your vision?

24:2 How will your faith apply to your vision-journey and how do you expect it to grow?

24:3 What does this project truly mean to you personally? Why is it important and what difference will it make in your life?

DAY 25
SUM IT UP

A man to carry on a successful business must have imagination. He must see things as in a vision, a dream of the whole thing. Charles M. Schwab, American Industrialist, Businessman

You've come a long way. I hope you haven't felt unduly overwhelmed or that your vision quest is impossible. It's not. Just keep it simple, avoid definition creep, and stick to the basics.

Summarize

I hope you have answered each chapter's questions in your own notebook. Those answers will be helpful to now summarize your plan into an executive summary. In business, this is a project synopsis composed of brief sentences or bullet points. The vision summary you will make is composed of your:

- **Current situation**
- **Vision**
- **Strategy**
- **Personal behaviors that need to change**
- **Forward-looking plan**
- **Product**
- **Market**
- **Production**
- **Delivery**
- **Administration**
- **Finances**
- **Targets and dates**
- **Accountability**
- **Spiritual implications**

As an example, I've included a model executive summary. In an earlier chapter, you read about Couple Number One—the retired pair who spent all their time taking vacations and playing golf. The summary that follows shows a redemptive vision they could be pursing. In fact, this is a modified version of one of my student's plans:

Sample Vision Summary:
Current Situation: *Am retired, debt-free, and a church member. I play golf, hold a university degree and have significant business experience. I have free time and am personally moved when I see the needs of people in the poorer parts of town.*

Vision: *To change lives in the inner city – spiritually, socially, and economically – by being a mentor and tutoring high-school students from poor families, thereby enabling them to graduate, get jobs and go to university. Will also develop a like-minded team who will join me in this work.*

Strategy:
1. **Personal behaviors to change:** *Cut down TV time, only play golf in the mornings, take vacations during school holidays*
2. **Forward plan:** *Develop concept and gain support of church leaders, school officials, parents while engaging a team of tutors*

Product: *Tutoring services to complement high-school courses, also involving personal counseling/encouragement and spiritual mentoring*

Market: *High-school students in the inner city*

Production: *In church classrooms, after school and early evenings, always at least two tutors onsite for accountability & safety*

Delivery: *One hour sessions, one-on-one*

Administration: *Need system for scheduling students and tutors, and for bookkeeping*

Finances: *Need school materials, books, and other tutors. Initially to be funded from personal sources. As program grows, will ask support from participating and interested churches.*

Targets and Dates
- *Meeting church elder/school principle, by next Friday*
- *Gain commitment of pastor/elders/parents, by end 1st month*
- *Start tutoring 3 students, by end of 2nd month*
- *Engage other tutors by end of 3rd month*
- *Expand to another church by end of 4th month*

Accountability: *John, a church leader & friend*

Spiritual Impact: *This is a redemptive work that I am personally excited about doing. In doing it, I can apply my interests and capabilities. My vision will make a big difference in people's lives and will have a long-term impact in a spiritual, social and economic reality.*

Final Assignment:
Go back through your notebook and write an executive summary of your vision and plan with these headings. Keep it between one and three pages.

My Vision Summary

Current Situation:

Vision:

Strategy
1. Personal behaviors to change:
2. Forward plan:

Product: What exactly is my product?

Market: Who is the market for my product?

Production: Where will my product be produced?

Delivery: How is my product distributed or delivered?

Administration: What organization and tools do I need? Do I need partners and what is our agreement? What does each person contribute to the project, and what does each person receive from the project?

Finances: What finances are required and where do they come from?

Targets and Dates: What are my major milestones and by when?

Accountability: To whom will I be accountable?

Spiritual Impact: How will your project redeem and advance the world? What are the spiritual implications to you personally? How might you grow in your faith in Jesus Christ through this project?

INTO THE JOURNEY

Do not follow where the path may lead. Go, instead, where there is no path and leave a trail. Anonymous

You've done it. You have identified your deepest desires and narrowed them down to one vital thing you want to happen at a definite point in the near future. You worked hard to assemble the plan and structure to bring your vision to life.

To close, I would like to leave you with a few thoughts. If they sound familiar, good. That means you've already internalized the visionary process.

Keep your eyes on your vision

Remember that vision is partly 'the act or power of seeing or imagination'. Keep your eyes open and on your vision. Keep your vision foremost in your sight and mind and heart.

Your vision is the essential goal that drives your life forward. Devote your time toward achieving it. Give it more of your mental space. If your busy life involves many responsibilities, then prioritize them in light of your vision, and commit to doing at least one thing every day that will support your vision.

Stay flexible

Just like you stretch your muscles for flexibility, keep your vision limber. Your plan is not set in stone. It is your best guess that will continually meet with reality now and in the future. Modify as you move forward. Stay innovative and constantly ask yourself if there is a better way to perform your current and coming tasks.

Stop living solely for your personal pleasure

Don't let yourself get caught in a purely pleasure-seeking cycle that ignores the suffering of those around you. As the greatest commandment said: love the Lord your God and your neighbor as yourself.

Remember your generic job description? God wants us to redeem this broken world. A good vision, one that matters, makes things better. It redeems. A good vision changes the system in a positive way. It is a recognition that God is Lord and that your vision fits within the inauguration of his kingdom on earth. And as a pleasant by-product, a good vision that changes your life and the lives of others will give you and its recipients great satisfaction.

Re-route the routine

I traveled through developing and established nations for many years. From Hong Kong to Sweden, I saw people continually performing the routines and patterns that their established social system valued. Routines are fine—as long as they don't prevent you from making a difference with your life. And routines are especially limiting if they stop you from doing what really matters. If you retire into a secure routine—whether you're twenty or sixty—your wrinkles won't come with much wisdom.

Journey in faith

Step out in faith.

I sincerely hope you do. I hope you achieve your quest. As you enter the unknown, remember that you will learn as you go along. In the end, things may turn out very differently than you originally envisioned—maybe even better. Most of all, I hope you grow in your faith on this journey. To conclude;

What is your vision?

You know it.

Now go for it.

RECOMMENDED READINGS

Banks, Robert. *Redeeming The Routines: Bringing Theology to Life.* Victor Books, 1993.

Guinness, Os. *The Call: Finding and Fulfilling the Central Purpose of your Life.* Word Publishing, 1998.

Hardy, Lee. *The Fabric of This World: Inquiries into Calling, Career Choice, and the Design of Human Work.* William B. Eerdmans Publishing Company, 1990.

Helm, Paul. *The Callings: The Gospel in the World.* The Banner of Truth Trust, 1987.

Mintzberg, Henry. *Strategy Safari: A Guided Tour Through the Wilds of Strategic Management.* Simon & Schuster, 1998.

Novak, Michael. *Business as a Calling: Work and the Examined Life.* The Free Press, 1996.

Schaeffer, Francis. *The God Who is There.* 30th anniversary ed. InterVarsity Press, 1998.

Schneider, John. *Godly Materialism: Rethinking Money & Possessions.* InterVarsity Press, 1994.

Smith, Gordon T. *Courage and Calling: Embracing Your God Given Potential.* InterVarsity Press, 1999.

Stevens, R. Paul. *The Other Six Days: Vocation, Work and Ministry in Biblical Perspective.* William. B. Eerdmans, 2000.

Warren, Rick. *The Purpose Driven Life: What on Earth am I Here For?* Zondervan, 2002.

END NOTES

1 Proverbs 29:18 (KJV).

2 www.sba.muohio.edu/pagecenter. This quote is also referenced on websites of various academic institutions.

3 Richard Cantillon, "*Essai Sur la Nature du Commerce en Général*", ("Essay on the Nature of Commerce") Paris, Institut National d'Etudes Démographiques, 1732.

4 Jean-Baptiste Say, *A Treatise on Political Economy, or the Production, Distribution and Consumption of Wealth*. This was first published in French in 1803 as *Traite d Economie Politique*. Five editions were published during Say s life, the last being in 1826. See Jean-Baptiste Say, *A Treatise on Political Economy: or the Production, Distribution, and Consumption of Wealth*, C.R. Prinsep and Clement C. Biddle, trans. (New York: Augustus M. Kelley, [1880] 1971), Page 111.

5 Joseph Schumpeter, *The Theory of Economic Development: An Inquiry into Profits, Capital, Credit, Interest and the Business Cycle*, (1911). See reprint edition, Somerset: Transaction Publishers, (January, 1983).

6 Alfred Marshall, *Principles of Economics: An Introductory Text*. See 8th edition, London: Porcupine Press, (June, 1949)

7 David McClelland, *The Achieving Society*, (Princeton: Van Nostrand: 1961).

8 www.business-plan.com.

9 Harold N. Shapiro, "Entrepreneurial Concepts, Definitions, and Model Formulations," *Entrepreneurship*, ed. Joshua Ronen (Lexington: Lexington Books, 1983), Page 77.

10 David Johnson, "What is Innovation and Entrepreneurship? Lessons for Larger Organisations," *Industrial and Commercial Training*," vol. 33, no. 4/5 (2001): Pages 135-140.

11 See note 1 above.

12 Peter Block, *The Answer to How Is Yes: Acting on What Matters*, (San Francisco: Berrett-Koehler, 2003), 194 pages.

13 John Calvin, *Institutes of the Christian Religion*, (Geneva, 1536), See 1559 translation edition, (Louisville: Westminster John Knox Press, June, 1960).

14 J.R.R. Tolkien, *The Lord of the Rings*, (Boston: Houghton Mifflin, 2005), 1216 pages.

15 Francis A. Schaeffer, *The God Who is There*, 30th Anniversary ed. (Downers Grove: InterVarsity Press, 1998), 226 pages.

16 Francis A. Schaeffer, "What was Job's mistake?" (sermon, l'Abri Fellowship, Huemoz Switzerland).

17 Henry Mintzberg, Joseph Lampel & Bruce Ahlstrand, *Strategy Safari: A Guided Tour Through the Wilds of Strategic Management*, (New York: Free Press; 1st edition. September 25, 1998), 416 pages.

18 R. E. Miles & C.C. Snow,(1978), *Organization Strategy, Structure, and Process*, (New York: McGraw-Hill, 1978) 274 pages. This is a highly referenced work in management literature and supports the theoretical foundation concerning the three questions. Also see their book, *Fit, Failure, and the Hall of Fame*, (New York, Free Press, 1994) which is an extension of their original work.

19 Gordon T. Smith, *On The Way: A Guide to Christian Spirituality*, (Colorado Springs: Navpress, 2001), Page 83.

20 John Schneider, *Godly Materialism: Rethinking Money & Possessions*, (Downers Grove: InterVarsity Press, 1994), Page 165.

21 Genesis 1:28.

22 II Thessalonians 3:10.

23 Doug Sherman and William Hendricks, *Your Work Matters to God*, (Colorado Springs: Navpress, 1987), Page 84.

24 Luke 12:15.

25 Luke 18:22.
26 Matthew 25: 26-30.

27 Donald Sull, "Disciplined Entrepreneurship," *MIT Sloan Management Review*, vol 46, Fall (2004).

28 Michal Novak, Business as Calling, (New York: The Free Press, 1996), Page 176

29 Paul Stevens, *The Other Six Days: Vocation, Work and Ministry in Biblical Perspective*, (Grand Rapids: William B. Eerdmans, 2000), Page 289.

30 William Tyndale, *Doctrinal Treatises*, ed. Henry Walker, (Cambridge: Cambridge University Press, 1848), Pages 98, 102.

31 Ulrich Zwingli, *On Mercenary Soldiers*, from a sermon about 1630, translated by John Cochran. Zwingli was born in 1484 and died in 1531, was educated at Bern, Vienna, and Basel and became Pastor of a church in Glarus, Switzerland, in 1506 and a Preacher at Zurich in 1518, where he inaugurated the Reformation.

32 See note 11 above.

33 William Perkins, *A Treatise of the Vocations or Callings of Men*, (1603), William Perkins, in Ian Breward, ed., *The Work of William Perkins* (Abingdon: The Sutton Courtenay Press, 1970), Pages 446-7.

Destinée Media

About the Author

Dr. Ralph McCall grew up in California and played as a professional basketball player in Israel, Europe, Asia, and Africa. He worked for a subsidiary organization of the World Trade Organization and the United Nations, and then as a manager in Hewlett-Packard, responsible for operations in Europe, Africa and the Middle-East. After leaving HP he worked with business partners in Switzerland with whom he started several companies. He has taught entrepreneurship courses and seminars at universities all over the world, and currently he is the director of several companies in Switzerland.

He has a Bachelor of Science degree from New York State University, an MBA from Henley Management College in the U.K., and a Doctorate in Business Administration from Brunel University in the U.K.

He bases himself in a small village in the Swiss Alps.

Vision to Life

This book is part of a growing series of guidebooks devoted to helping readers gain new insights into areas of practical living, such as entrepreneurship, ownership, vocation, and other topics. They systematically develop foundational principles, and then present reflective questions that enable you to 'Bring Your Vision to Life.' For more information go to, www.visiontolife.org

Destinée Media

This is a Destinée Media publication. Destinée aims to bring a fresh perspective to living, culture and worldviews. We publish both fiction and nonfiction, many of our works dealing with themes of theology, spirituality and Christian living.

We thank you for your interest in our materials and hope that you find them both relevant and challenging.

For more information please go to: www.destineemedia.com

www.ingramcontent.com/pod-product-compliance
Lightning Source LLC
Chambersburg PA
CBHW022334300426
44109CB00040B/602